I Can Draw...
Flying Machines

Artwork by Terry Longhurst

Text by Amanda O'Neill

This is a Parragon Publishing Book
This edition published in 2003

Parragon Publishing
Queen Street House
4 Queen Street
Bath BA1 1HE, UK

Designed, packaged, and produced by
Touchstone

ISBN 1-40540-019-6

Artwork by Terry Longhurst
Text by Amanda O'Neill
Edited by Philip de Ste. Croix

Printed in Dubai,U.A.E

About this book

Everybody can enjoy drawing, but sometimes it's hard to know where to begin. The subject you want to draw can look very complicated. This book shows you how to start, by breaking down your subject into a series of simple shapes.

The tools you need are very simple. The basic requirements are paper and pencils. Very thin paper wears through if you have to rub out a line, so choose paper that is thick enough to work on. Pencils come with different leads, from very hard to very soft. Very hard pencils give a clean, thin line which is best for finishing drawings. Very soft ones give a thicker, darker line. You will probably find a medium pencil most useful.

If you want to color in your drawing, you have the choice of paints, colored inks, or felt-tip pens. Fine felt-tips are useful for drawing outlines, thick felt-tips are better for coloring in.

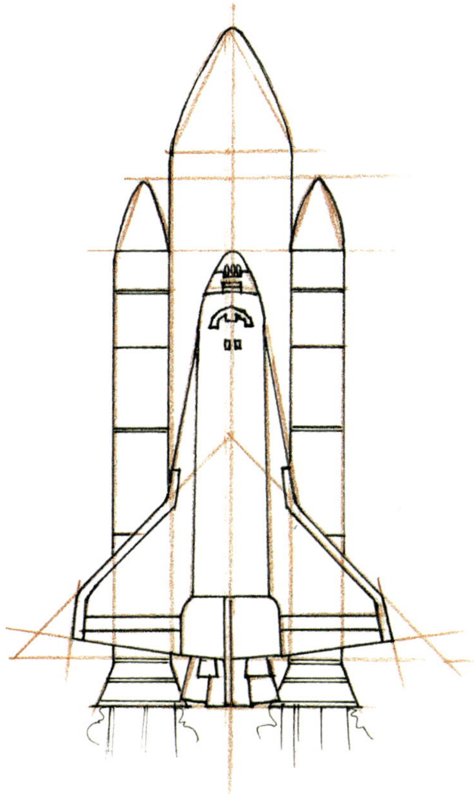

The most important tool you have is your own eyes. The mistake many people make is to draw what they think something looks like, instead of really looking at it carefully first. Half the secret of making your drawing look good is getting the proportions right. Study your subject before you start, and break it down in your mind into sections. Check how much bigger, or longer, or shorter, one part is than another. Notice where one part joins another, and at what angle. See where there are flowing curves, and where there are straight lines.

The step-by-step drawings in this book show you exactly how to do this. Each subject is broken down into easy stages, so you can build up your drawing one piece at a time. Look carefully at each shape before - and after - you draw it. If you find you have drawn it the wrong size or in the wrong place, correct it before you go on. Then the next shape will fit into place, and piece-by-piece you can build up a fantastic picture.

Harrier

This fighter plane is a jump jet – an aircraft which can take off straight upward, and land by coming straight down. It is designed for use on aircraft carriers, or anywhere there is limited space for a runway.

This triangle forms the wings.

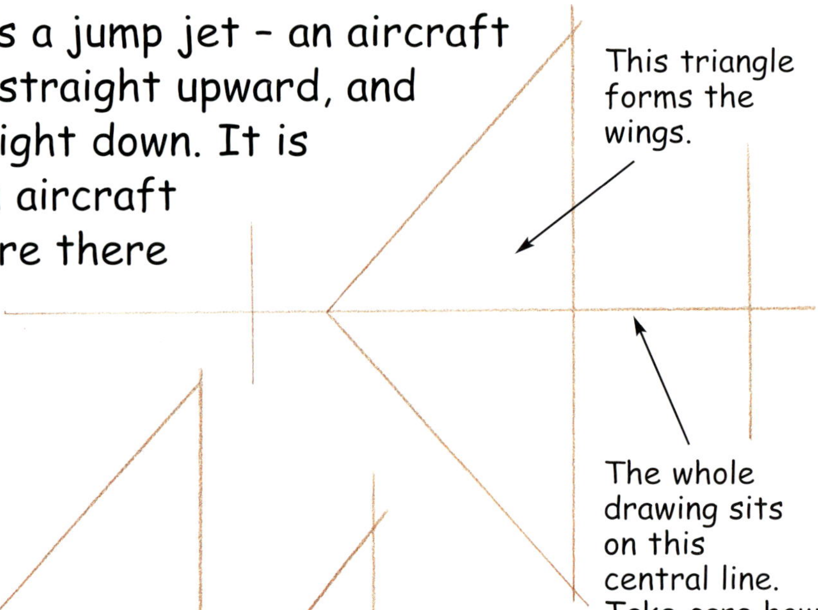

The whole drawing sits on this central line. Take care how you space your sections along it.

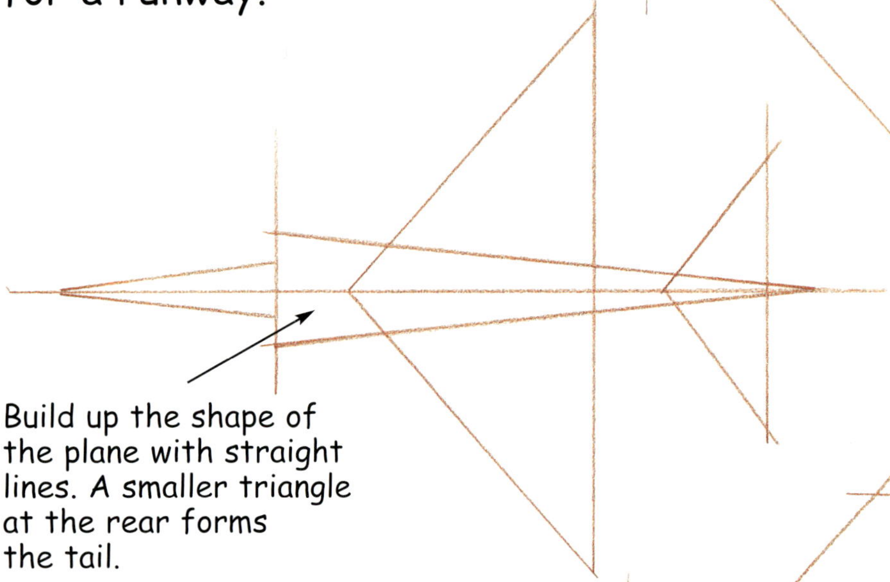

Build up the shape of the plane with straight lines. A smaller triangle at the rear forms the tail.

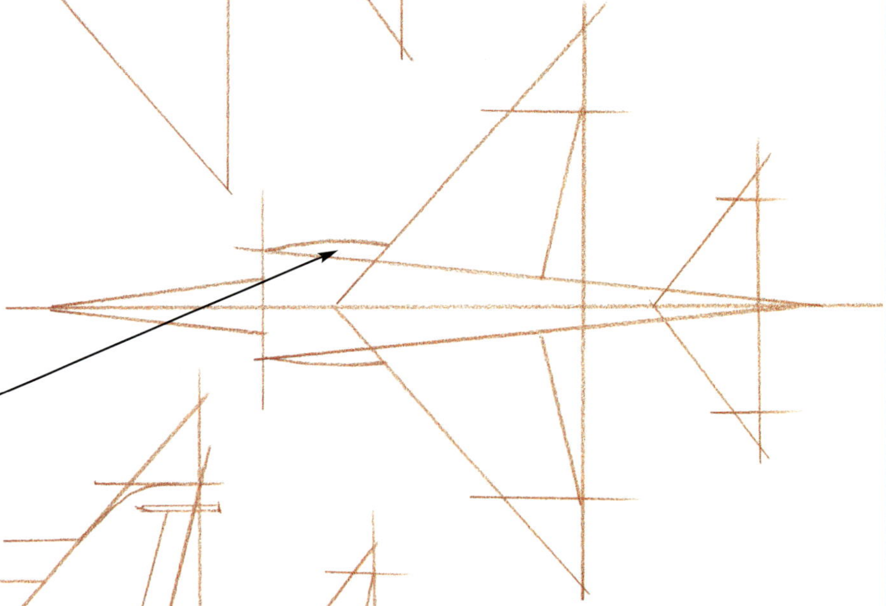

Now add a gentle curve on either side of the fuselage in front of the wings. This shapes the inlets that direct air to the engine.

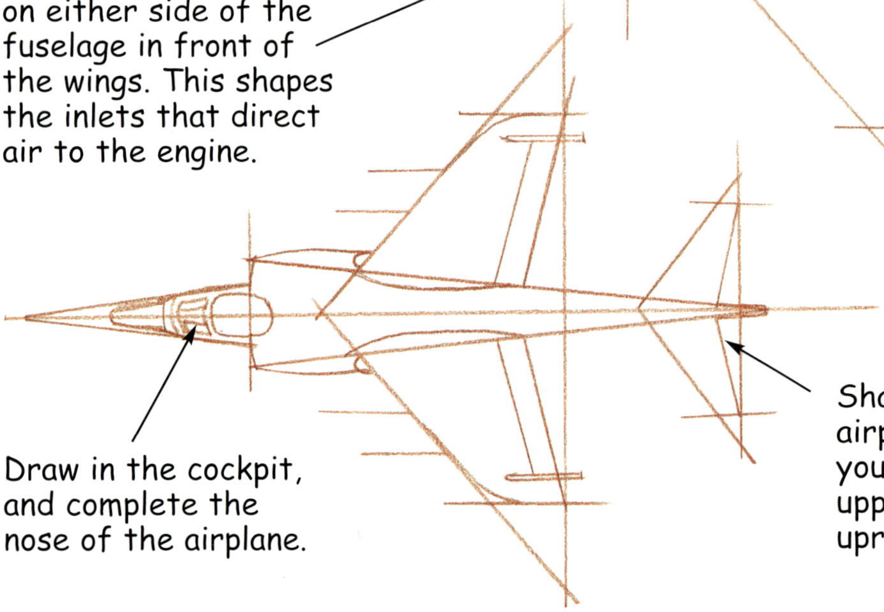

Draw in the cockpit, and complete the nose of the airplane.

Shape the tail of the airplane. From above, you can only see the upper edge of the upright tail fin.

The cockpit contains an ejector seat, so the pilot can escape quickly if the plane is in trouble.

Draw in camouflage markings, which make the aircraft harder for enemy planes to spot. Add roundels on the wings.

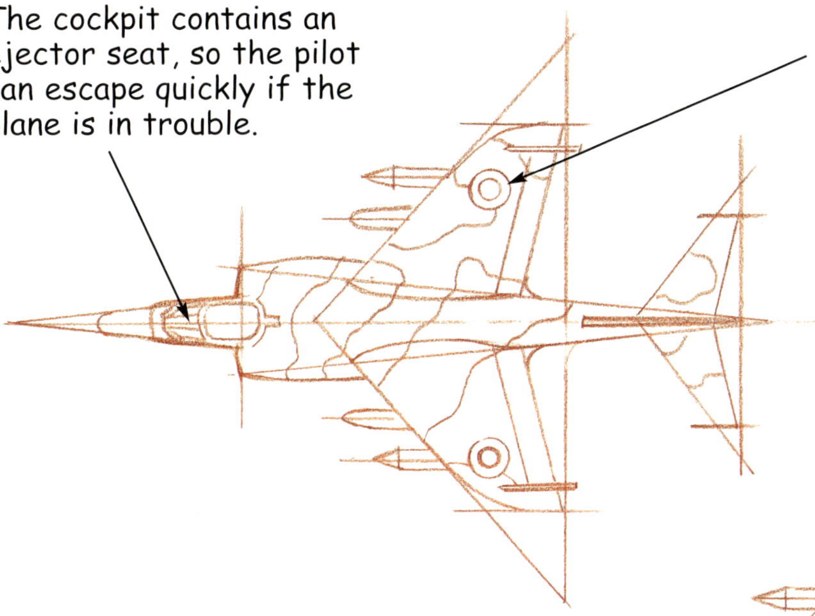

The Harrier's missiles and bombs and extra fuel tanks are carried under the wings.

The cockpit houses all the dials and controls that help the pilot to fly.

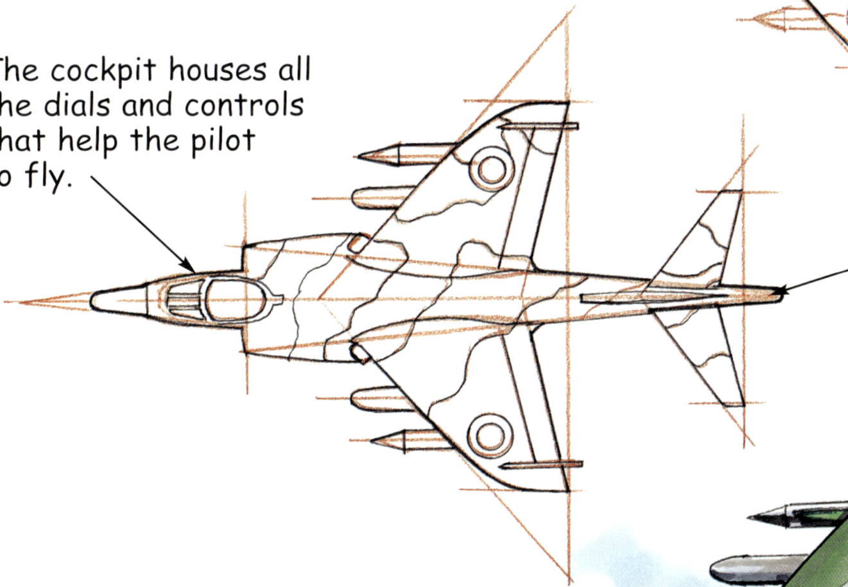

This is the radar warning receiver, to spot enemy aircraft coming up behind.

The Harrier is the only Vertical Take-Off and Landing (VTOL) fighter in service in the western world. It works because the engine nozzles can swivel to point downward when it is time to take off or land.

Avro Tutor

This little biplane was used in the 1930s to train military pilots. A basic trainer for absolute beginners, it flies very slowly and is therefore easy to land. It has two seats, one for the learner pilot and one for the instructor. Pilots learned the basic skills on this before moving on to faster aircraft.

These three shapes form the body (fuselage) of the plane and its upright tail fin.

Now add the flat tailplane, with its squared-off ends, under the upright fin.

These two small circles form the wheels.

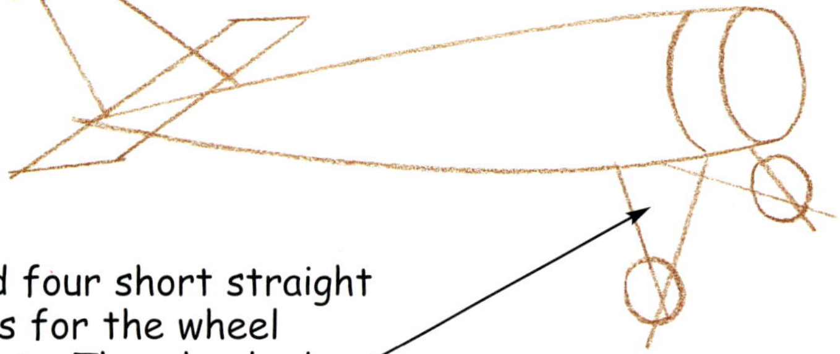

Add four short straight lines for the wheel struts. The wheels do not fold away, but hang down when the aircraft is in flight.

Draw the two pairs of wings, of the same size, one above the other.

The wings are made of fabric, stretched over a framework of wood or metal.

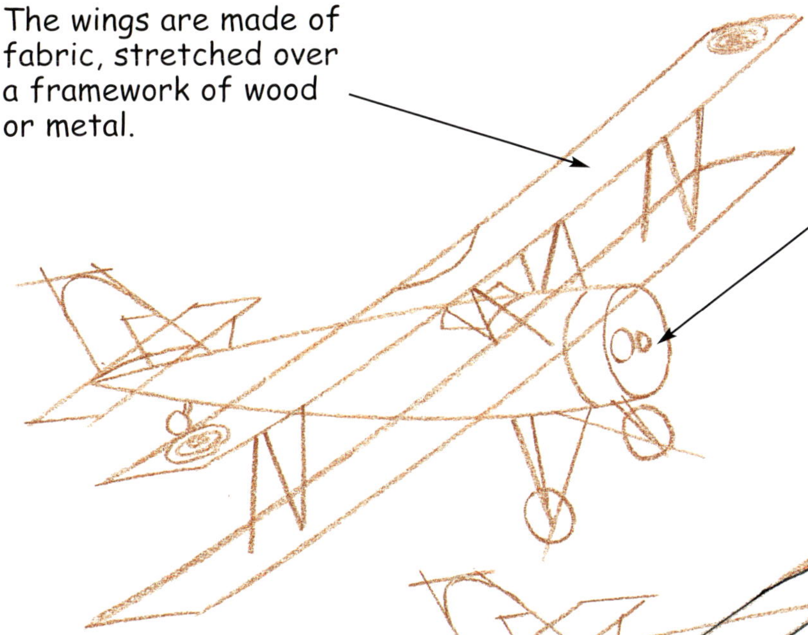

Draw in two small circles here for the visible parts of the engine, and the place where the propeller fits on.

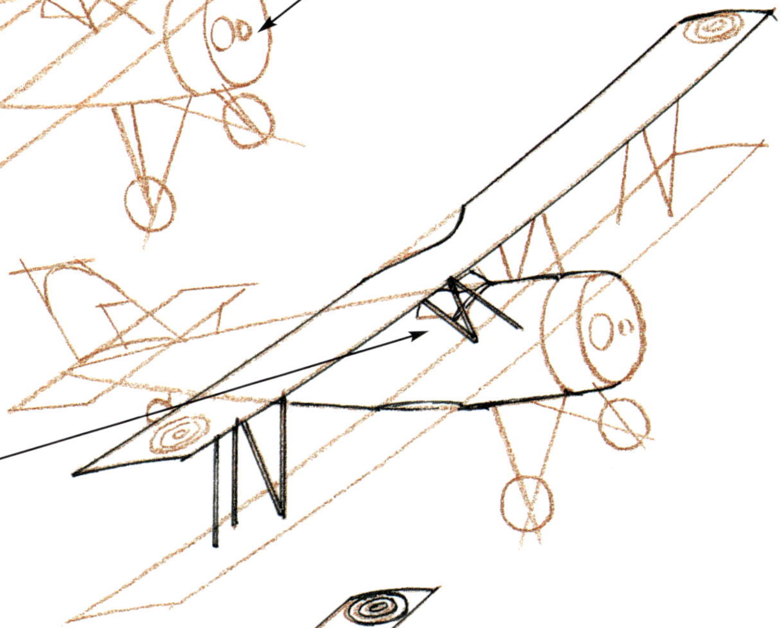

The open cockpit is very cold and drafty. In very cold countries like Canada, a canopy was fitted to give the pilot some protection.

The two pairs of wings are connected by slender struts, usually of wood, which are stronger than they look.

Aircraft like this, with wood and fabric wings, were jokingly said to be held together by 'sticks and string.'

Sunderland Flying Boat

The Sunderland was designed to travel over water as well as through the air. It was useful for long-range work, as it could stay in the air for more than 12 hours. It served with Britain's RAF from 1938 to 1955.

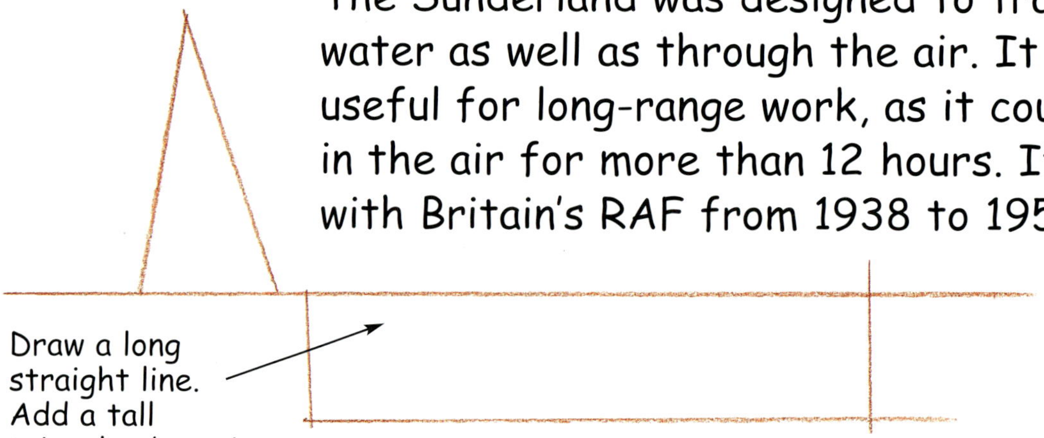

Draw a long straight line. Add a tall triangle above it at one end, and a long rectangle below it. These simple shapes form most of the plane.

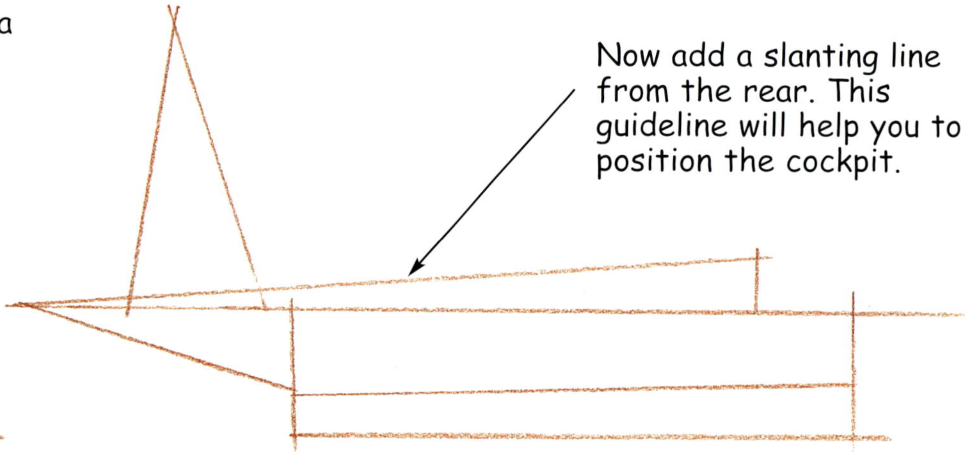

Now add a slanting line from the rear. This guideline will help you to position the cockpit.

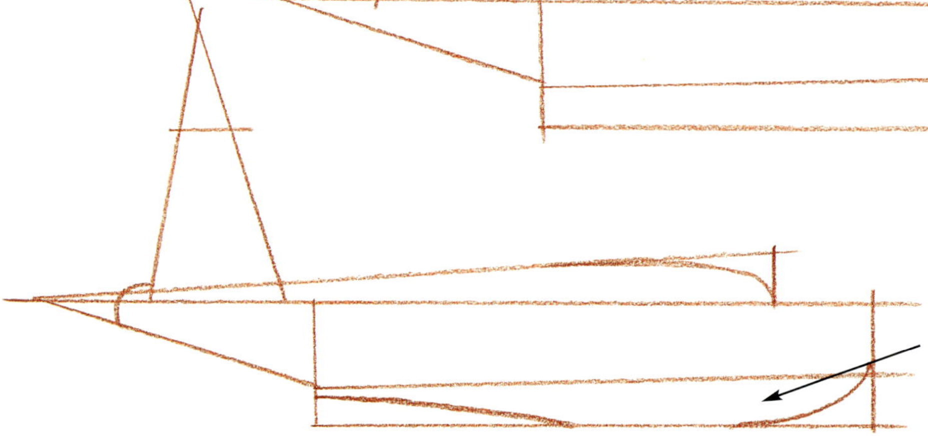

The hull is rounded, like that of a boat. It is designed not only to float, but to take off and land on water.

Round off the back of the aircraft and the tip of the tail. Although we use straight lines to start drawing this plane, it is made up of smooth curves.

Now draw in the cockpit at the front.

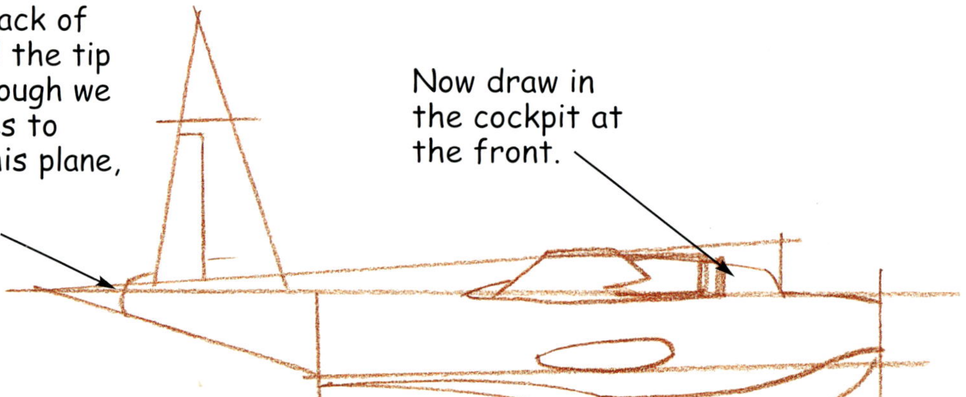

Just behind the wings, draw this gun turret, housing two machine guns and a gunner.

Add the front gun turret. This is power-operated, and contains four machine guns.

A flying boat has an internal, central float which is combined with the body of the plane.

This craft was developed from an airliner design – as you might guess from its shape. It is large and carries a big crew.

Neatly ink in the rows of portholes, and other details such as the RAF roundel marking.

The Sunderland carried so many machine guns – back, front, and center – that enemy pilots in World War II nicknamed it the 'Porcupine.'

Hot-air Balloon

This is the oldest form of flying machine, invented in France in 1783. It is also the simplest, using the natural law that hot air is lighter than cold air and therefore rises. It has no steering mechanism, but goes where the wind takes it.

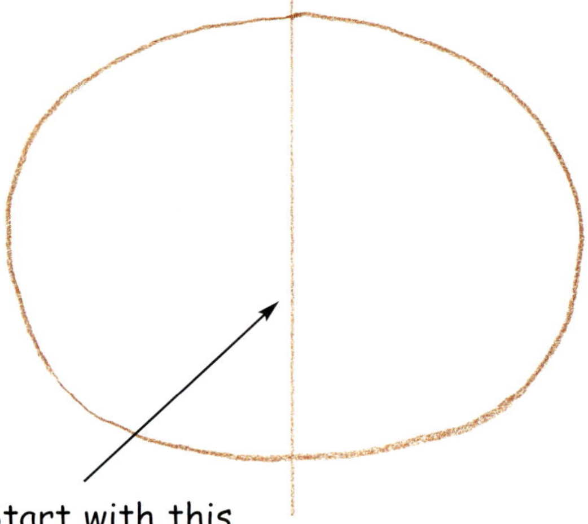

Start with this simple oval shape, and draw a straight line down the center.

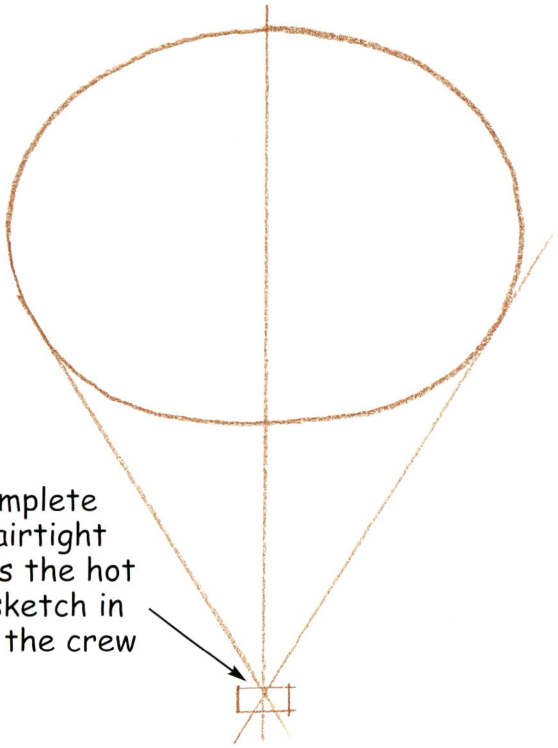

Two more lines complete the shape of the airtight canopy which holds the hot air. At the base, sketch in the basket where the crew are stationed.

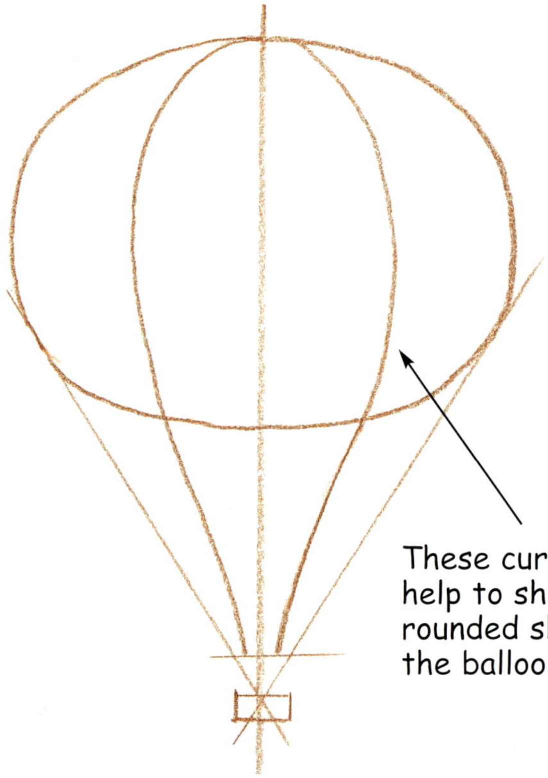

These curved lines help to show the rounded shape of the balloon.

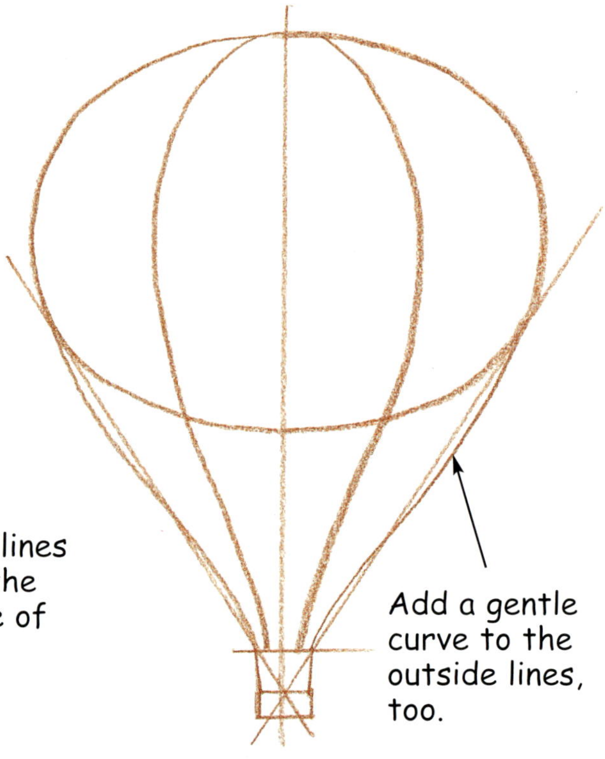

Add a gentle curve to the outside lines, too.

The balloon's bag, or envelope, is made of tough material, such as nylon, which will not rip apart in high winds.

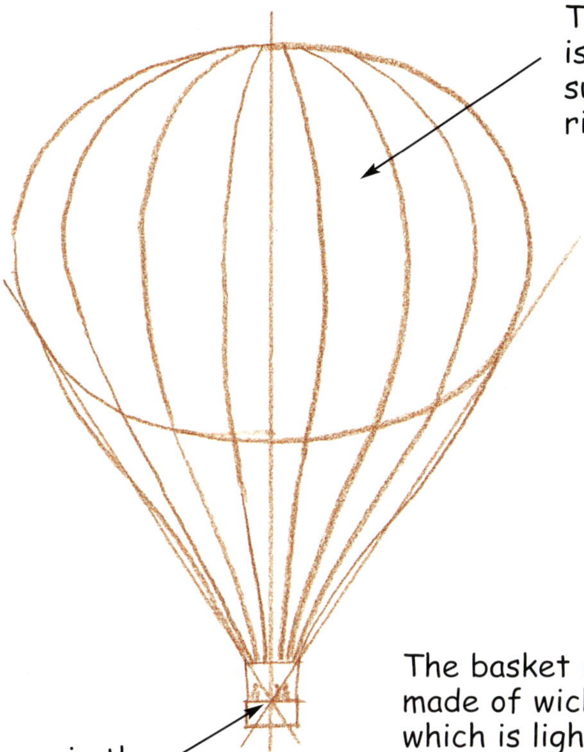

Draw in the basket, with the crew inside.

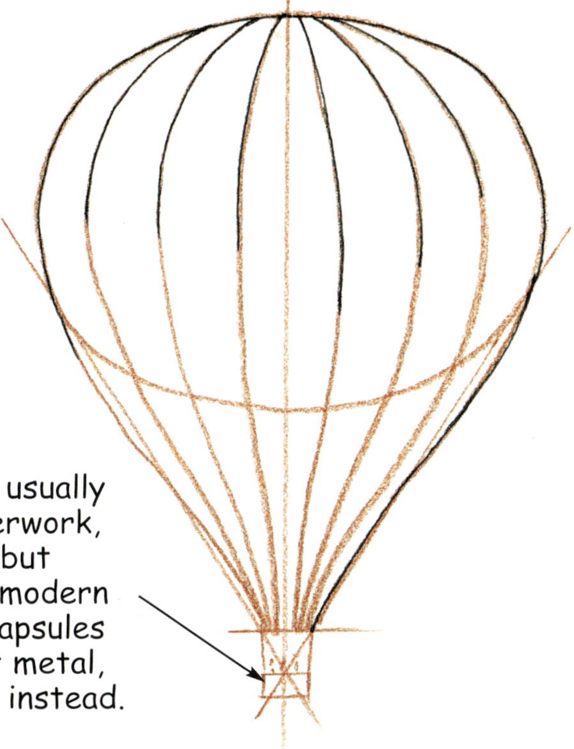

The basket is usually made of wickerwork, which is light but strong. Some modern balloons use capsules of lightweight metal, like aluminum, instead.

Above the crew's heads, a gas burner, rather like a giant camping stove, creates the hot air.

Gulfstream

This American twin-jet airplane can carry up to 19 passengers in comfort. It is also used for special duties from anti-submarine warfare to sea and fishery patrols.

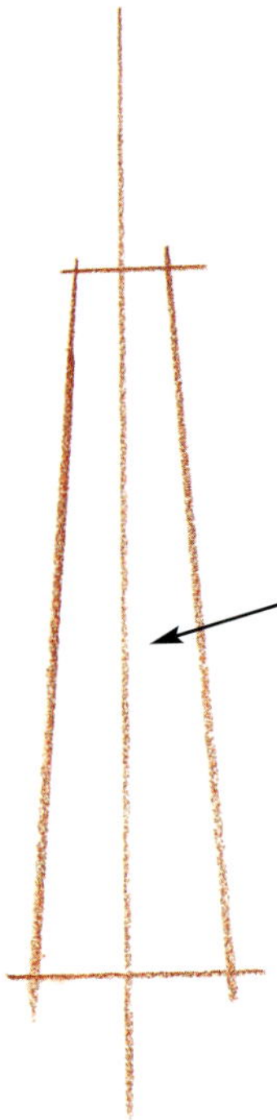

Start with this rectangular shape across a central line.

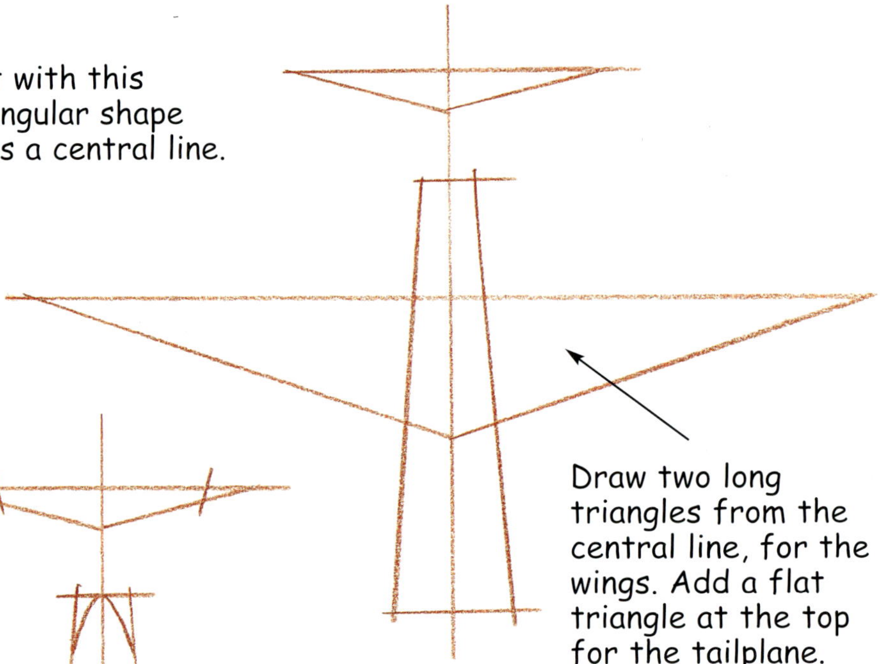

Draw two long triangles from the central line, for the wings. Add a flat triangle at the top for the tailplane.

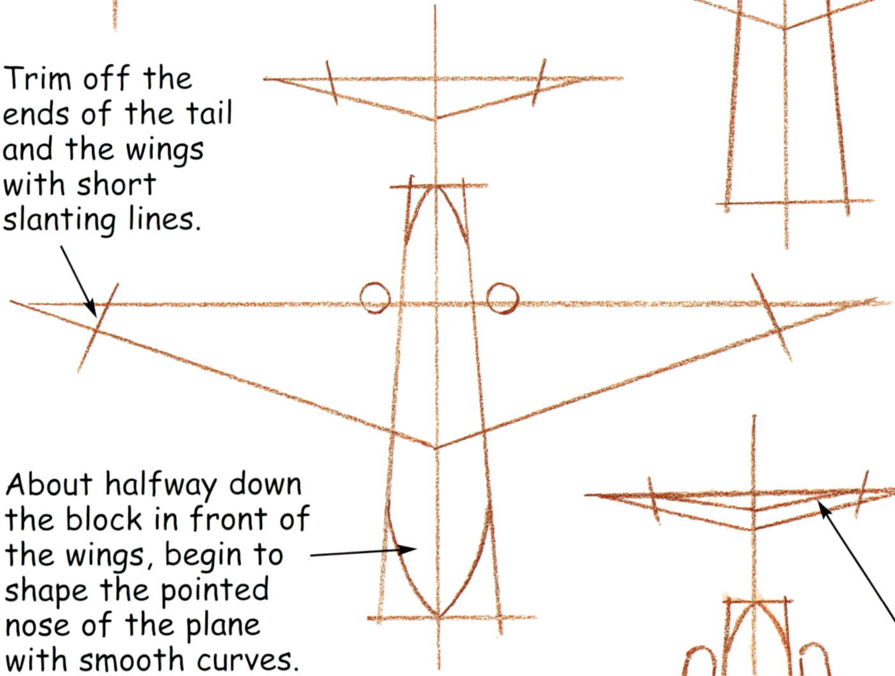

Trim off the ends of the tail and the wings with short slanting lines.

About halfway down the block in front of the wings, begin to shape the pointed nose of the plane with smooth curves.

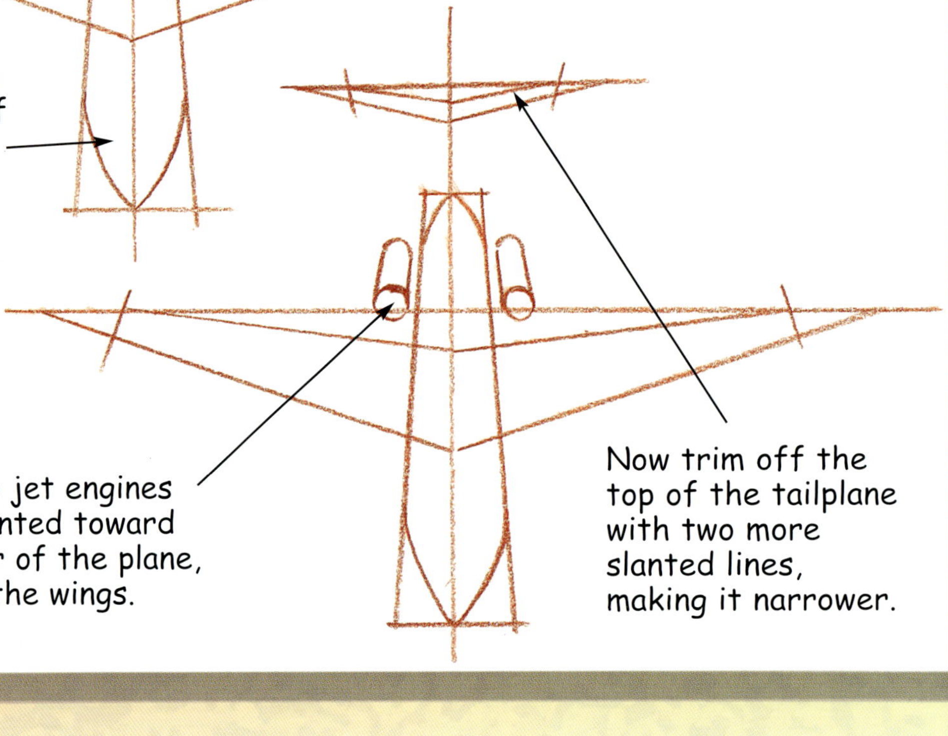

The two jet engines are mounted toward the rear of the plane, behind the wings.

Now trim off the top of the tailplane with two more slanted lines, making it narrower.

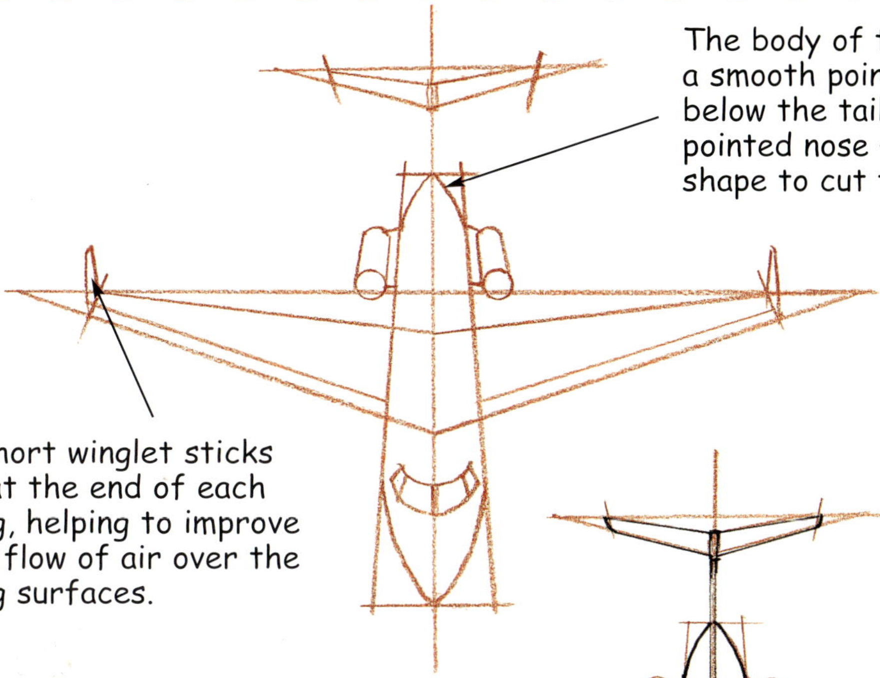

The body of the plane comes to a smooth point at the rear, just below the tail, matching the pointed nose – a streamlined shape to cut through the air.

A short winglet sticks up at the end of each wing, helping to improve the flow of air over the wing surfaces.

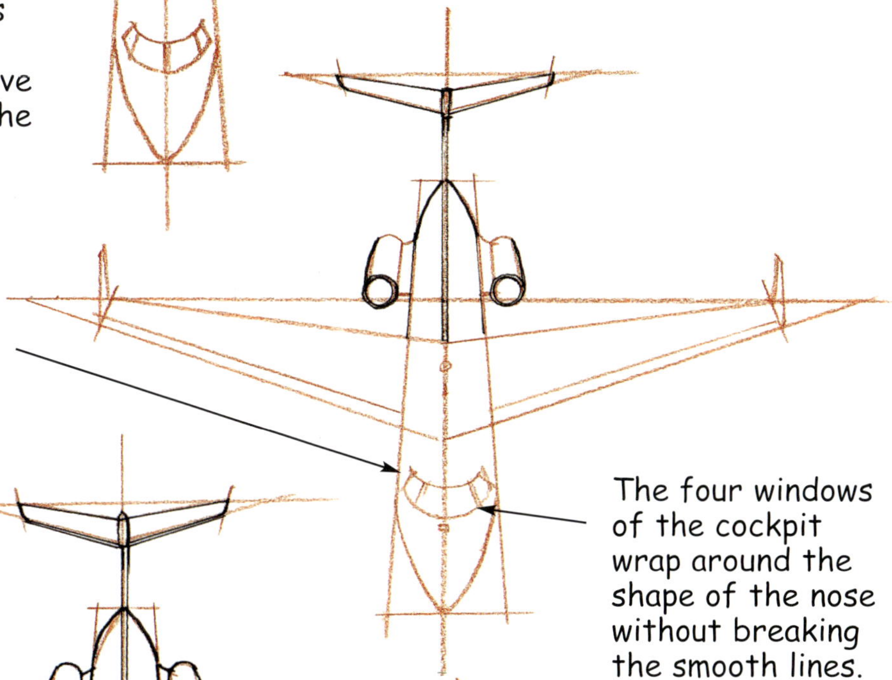

The cockpit holds two pilots, and there is room for a flight attendant as well as passengers in the main cabin.

The four windows of the cockpit wrap around the shape of the nose without breaking the smooth lines.

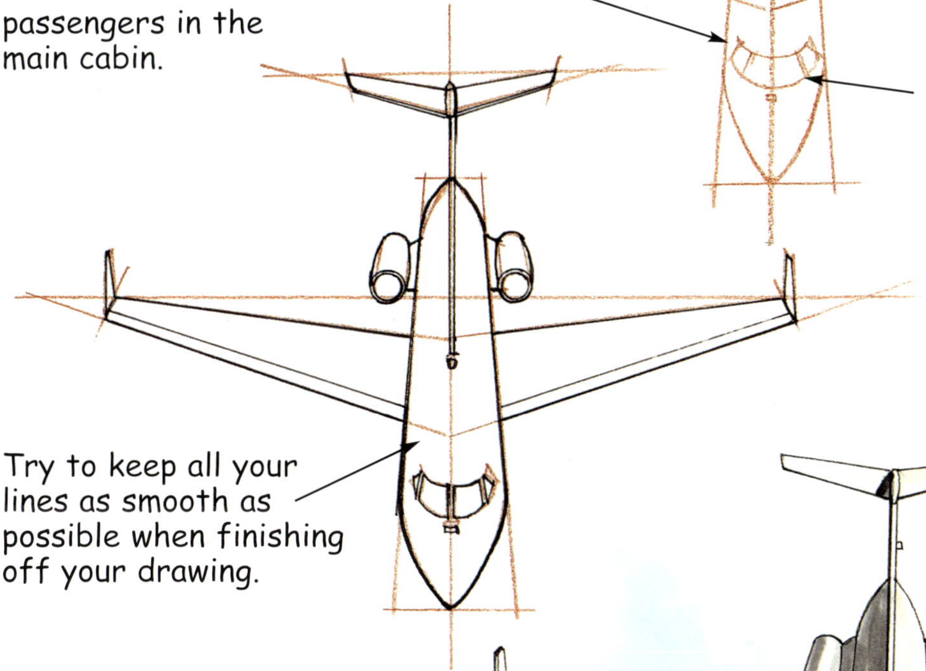

Try to keep all your lines as smooth as possible when finishing off your drawing.

The Gulfstream is a luxurious aircraft that provides transport for VIPs (very important persons), like film stars or top business people.

Bulldog

The Bulldog is a trainer airplane for learner pilots, and it can also be used as a ground-attack aircraft. It is usually unarmed, but can carry guns, bombs, or missiles under the wings. It first flew in 1969, and is in service with six air forces.

These two simple shapes – an oblong and a triangle – are the starting point.

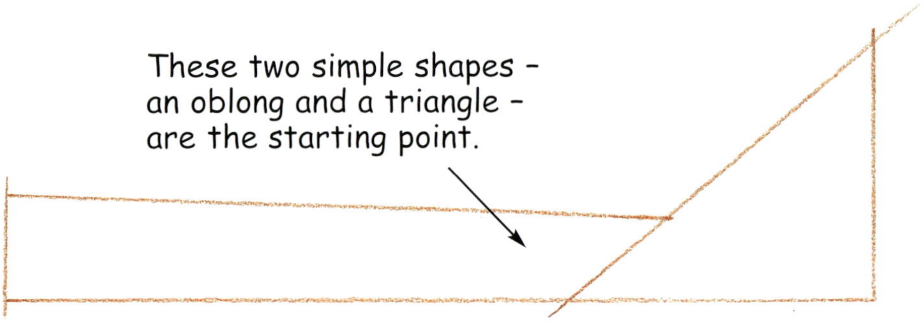

Draw a long smooth curve for the cockpit. Follow this up with a slanting line along the whole body from nose to tail.

A dividing line helps you to draw the characteristic tail shape.

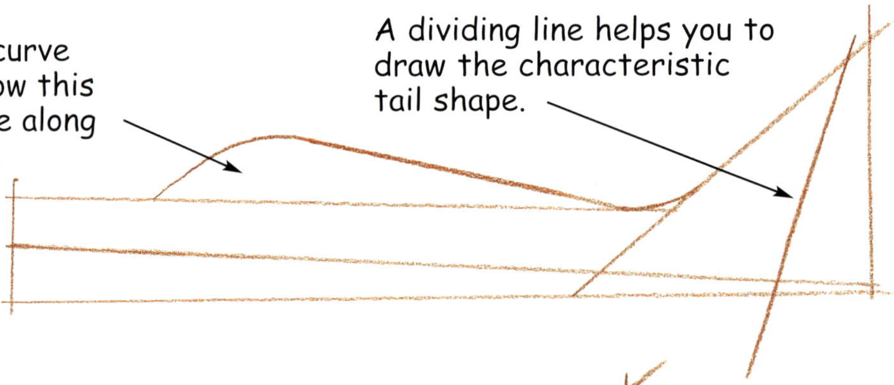

This shape forms the wing nearest you.

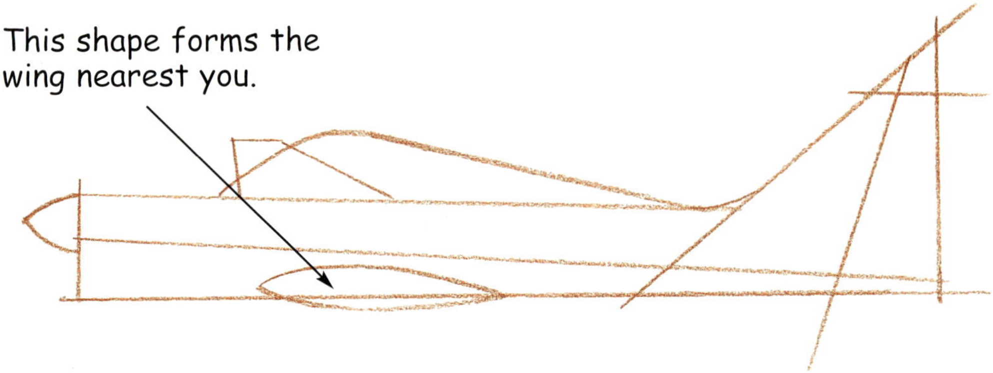

Draw the front wheel. The Bulldog has three wheels, but only this one can be folded away in flight.

The cockpit is a big glass 'bubble,' so that the pilot can see all around.

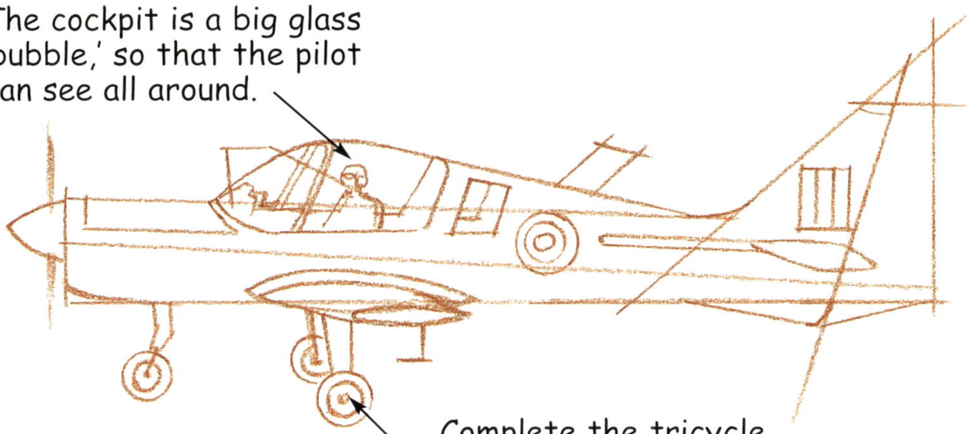

Complete the tricycle undercarriage with two back wheels.

Finish drawing the pilot. On a training flight, the trainer pilot and instructor sit side by side with an observer behind them.

Notice how the aircraft has rather a hump-backed look to allow room for the crew members to fit inside.

Shape the top of the tail fin so that it is squared off.

This small plane is of all-metal construction. Like most trainer aircraft, it is quite a slow flier – its maximum speed is about 150mph.

Hang Glider

A hang glider is like a big kite, strong enough to carry the weight of a man hanging beneath it.

Start with a large triangle, divided by a slanting line. This forms the large, fabric-covered frame.

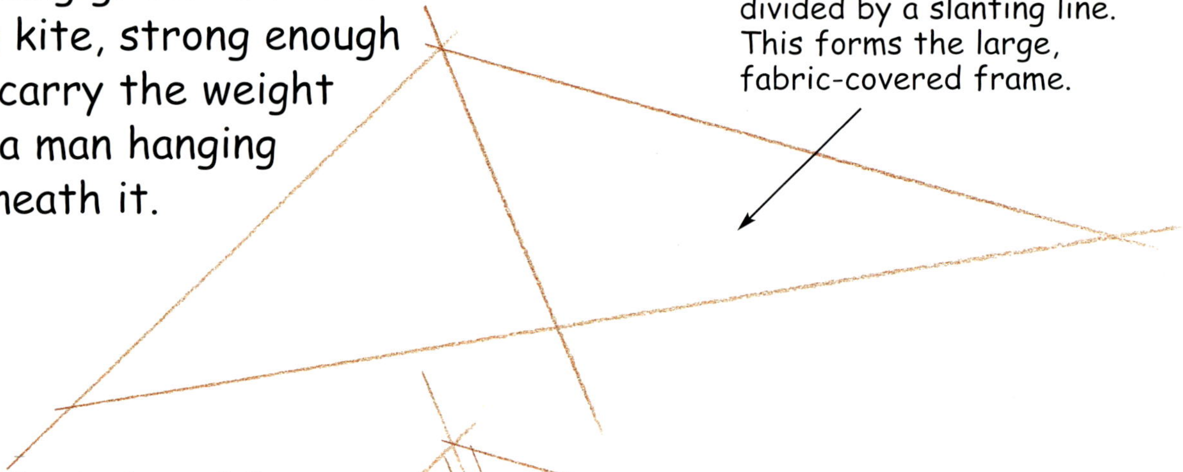

The front edges of the fabric covering are doubled over to make them stronger.

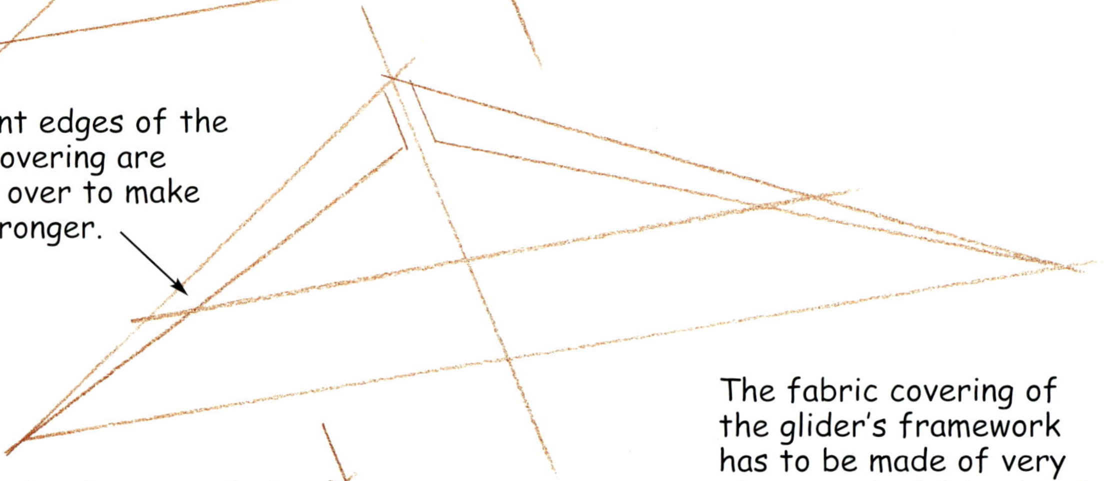

The fabric covering of the glider's framework has to be made of very strong material to stand up to high winds.

Draw a triangle suspended from the central point. This is a light hanging frame which the pilot holds.

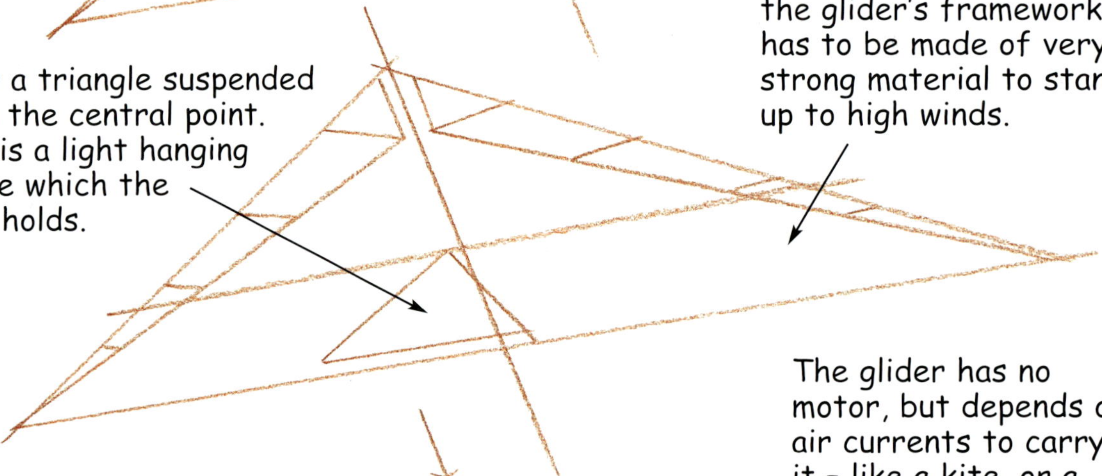

The glider has no motor, but depends on air currents to carry it – like a kite, or a gliding bird.

The pilot hangs from a harness attached to the framework, and grips the control bar with his hands.

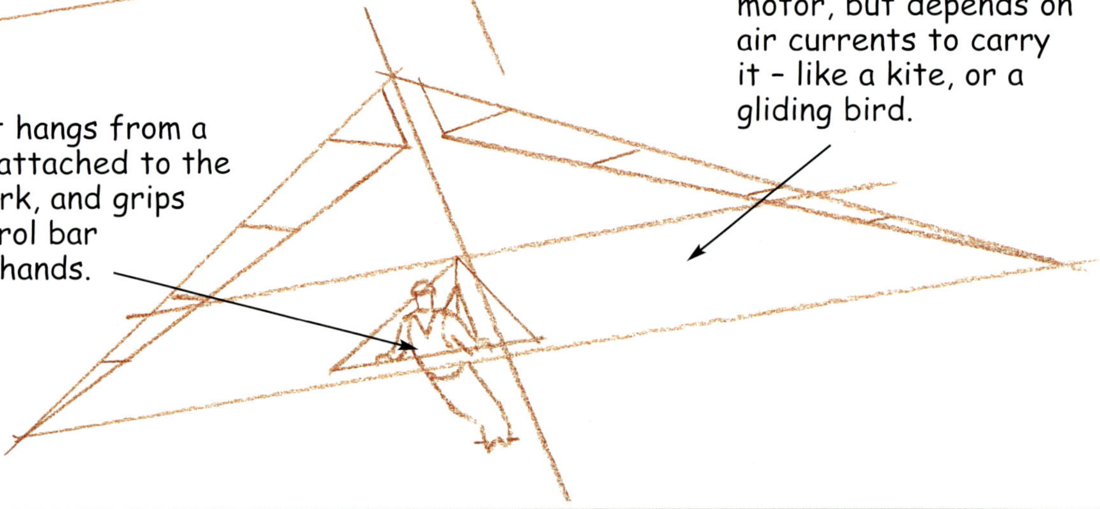

Use straight lines to draw in the wing struts, clearly visible under the fabric cover.

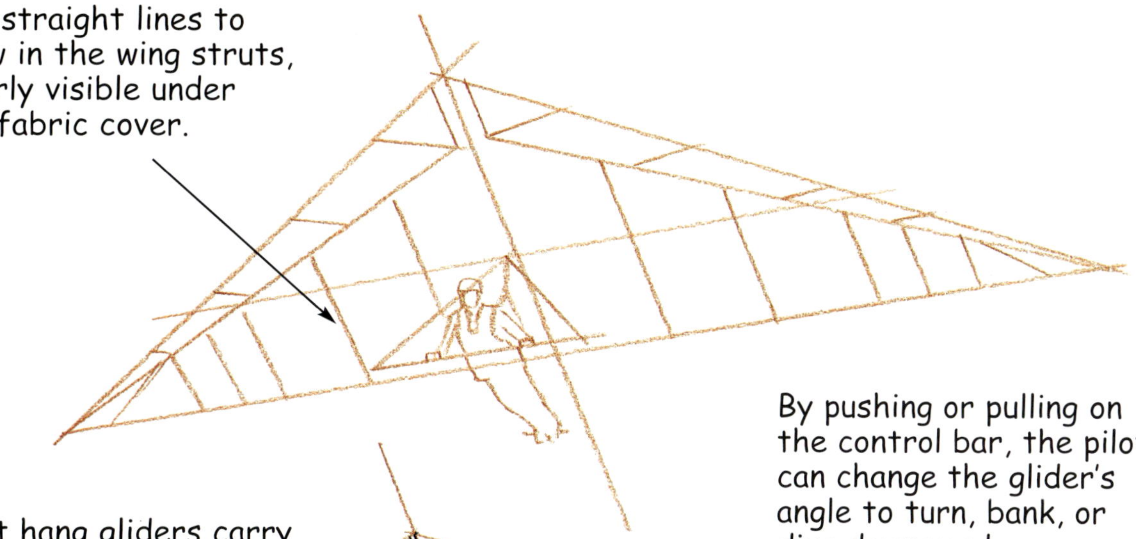

By pushing or pulling on the control bar, the pilot can change the glider's angle to turn, bank, or dive downward.

Most hang gliders carry only one person, the pilot. But some can take a passenger as well.

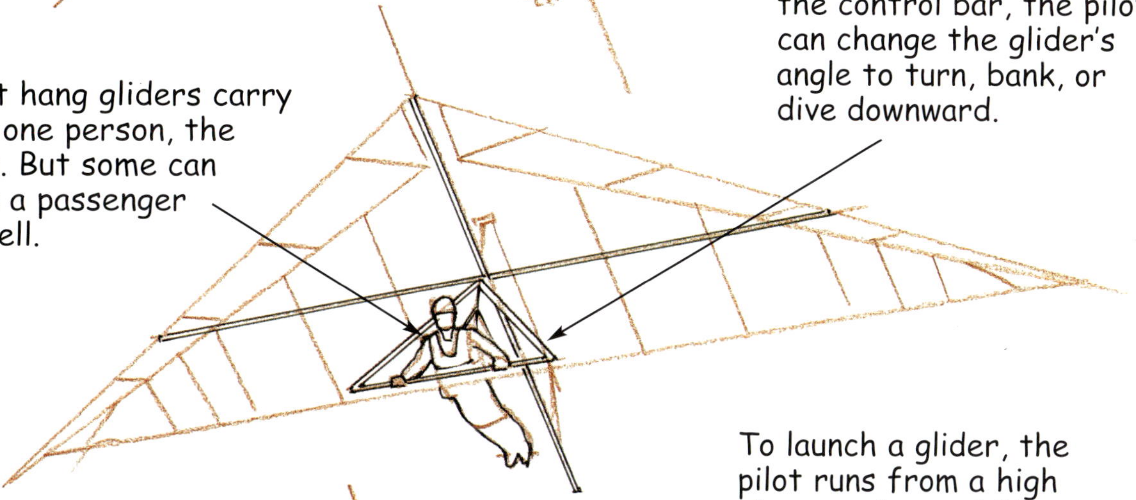

To launch a glider, the pilot runs from a high place, such as a hilltop, into the wind. Rising air currents lift him upward.

Hang gliders are often gaily colored – for safety reasons, so they show up at a distance.

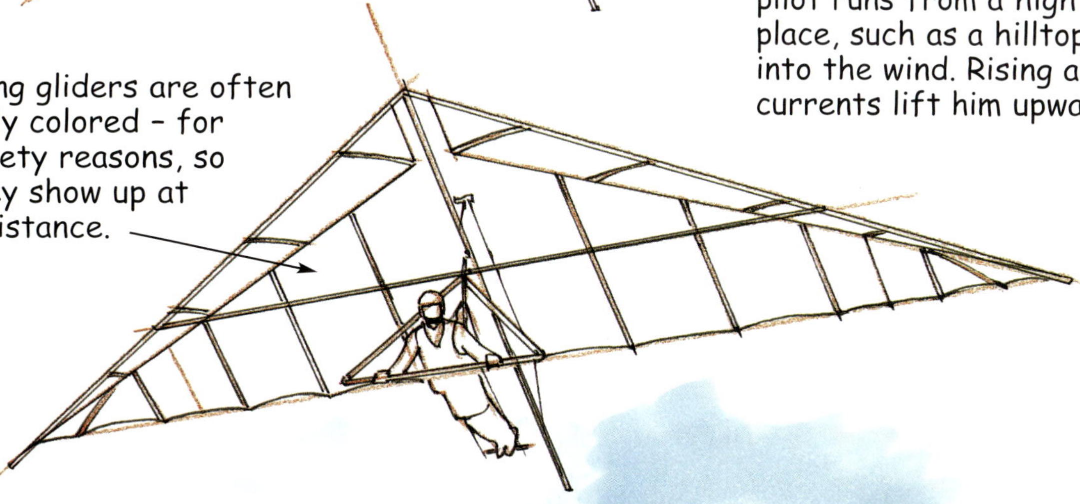

Hang gliding was pioneered in Germany in the 1890s. But it did not become popular until the 1960s. Today hang-glider races are often held along high mountain ranges.

F-14 Tomcat

This fighter plane was specially designed to fly from aircraft carriers. Its task is to attack other fighter planes, and also to take on enemy bombers.

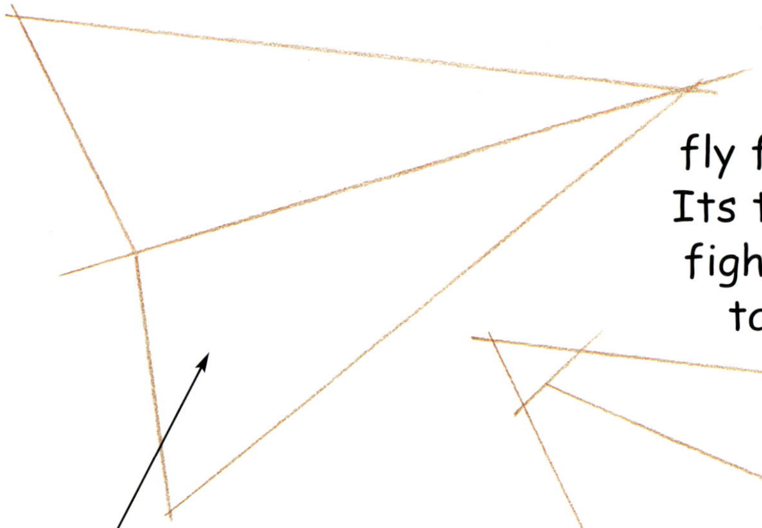

Start with a central line and two triangles for the wings – a shape rather like a paper airplane.

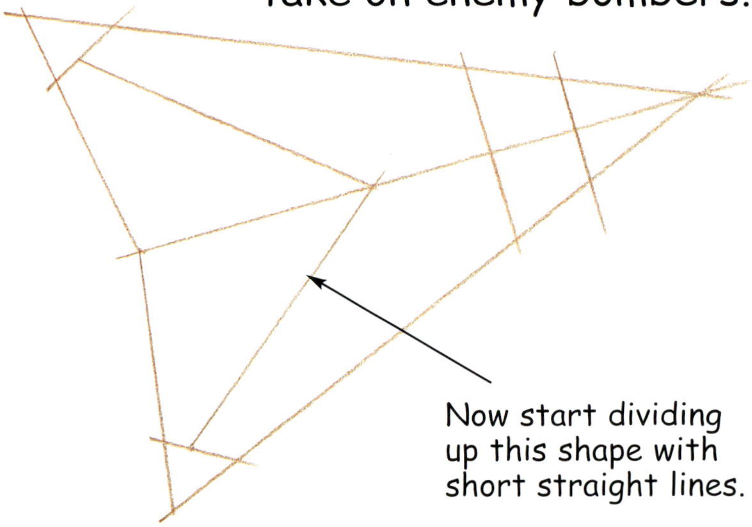

Now start dividing up this shape with short straight lines.

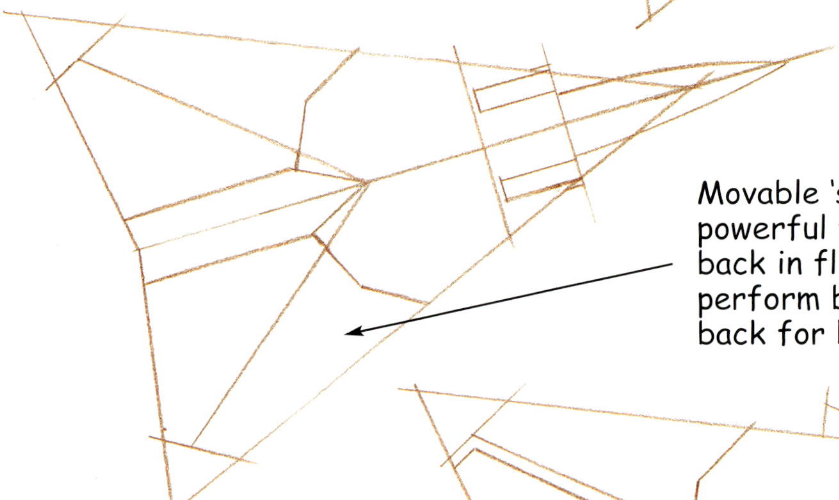

Movable 'swing wings' fitted with powerful flaps and slats can fold back in flight to make the plane perform better. They swing right back for high-speed flight.

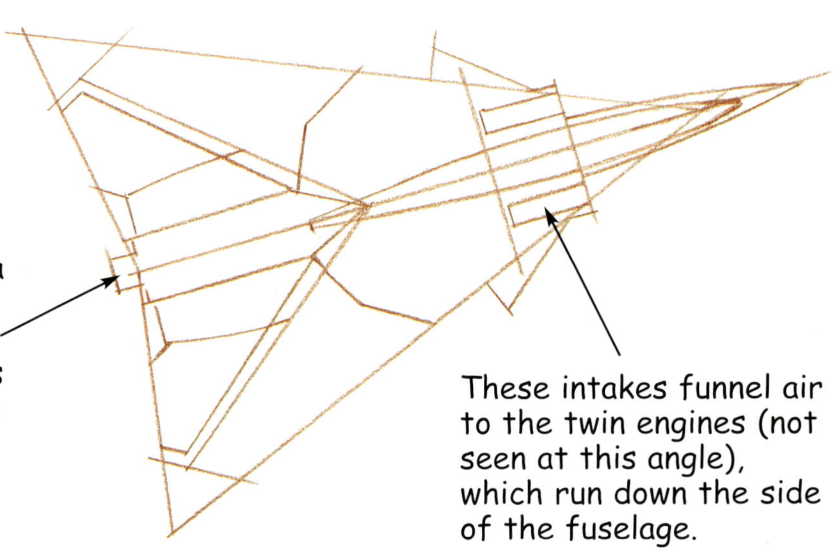

Draw the radar 'stinger' as a small oblong. Called a stinger because it is set at the tail like a wasp's sting, it warns of missiles or enemy aircraft coming up from behind.

These intakes funnel air to the twin engines (not seen at this angle), which run down the side of the fuselage.

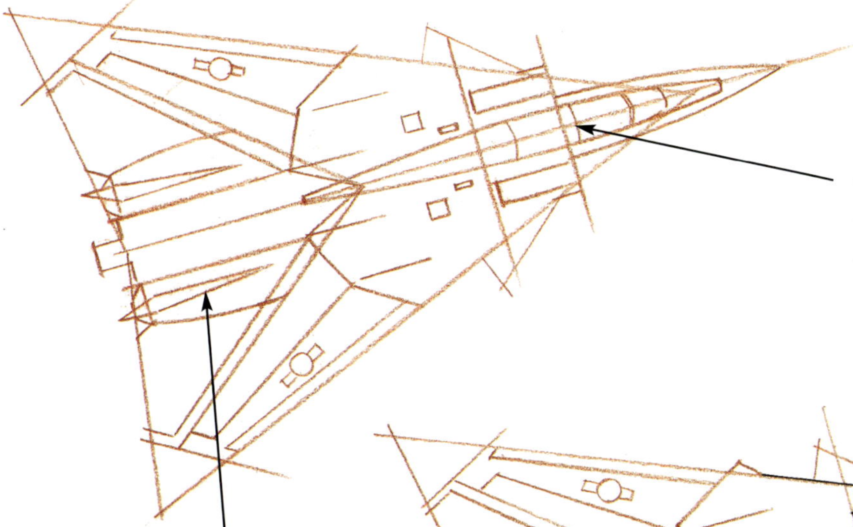

The central cockpit houses a full range of up-to-date electronics equipment. The weapons systems officer sits behind the pilot.

Continue to develop the shape of the body at the back. It looks complicated, but it is all built up from simple lines. Note how the wings line up with the tailplanes.

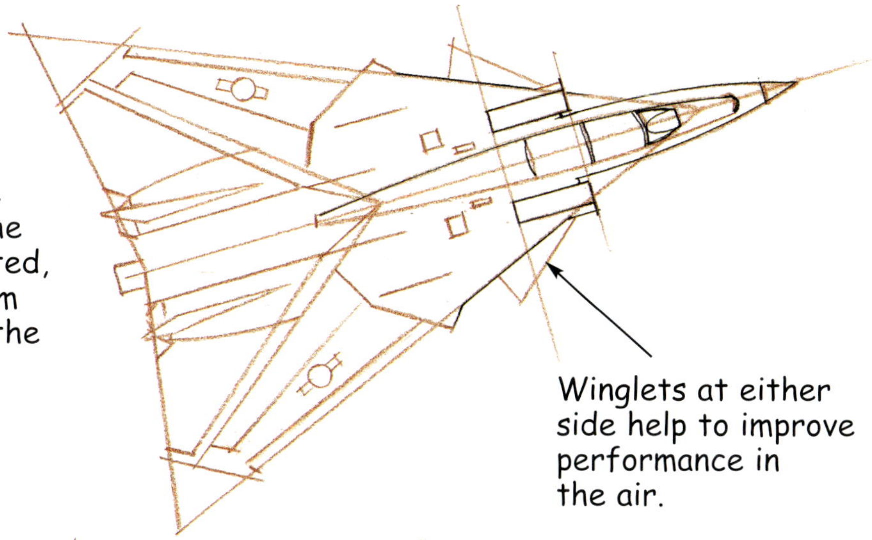

Winglets at either side help to improve performance in the air.

The Tomcat is heavily armed, with a wide range of attack weapons including air-to-air missiles, and a multi-barrel gun.

The Tomcat is the aircraft flown by the US Navy's 'top guns' – its elite fighter pilots.

Mustang

One of fastest aircraft of World War II, this fighter plane was so highly thought of that it was nicknamed the 'Cadillac of the Air' after the famous car. It first flew in 1940. Designed in America, it was used to escort bombers from Britain on their long-range missions over Germany.

Start with the body of the airplane and a narrow triangle for the tail fin.

One straight line and one bent one form the guidelines for the wings.

Now draw the nose cone – termed a 'spinner' because it spins round and round with a propeller attached.

Square off the tail at the top.

Now add a low curve at the center of your top line for the small glass canopy.

The Mustang has square-ended wings, matching the squared-off tail.

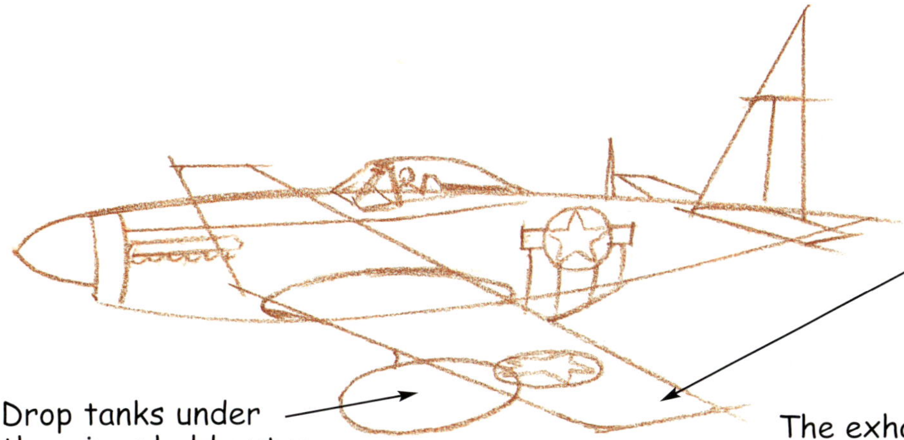

Drop tanks under the wings hold extra fuel, allowing the Mustang to fly farther. It was the only fighter that could escort bombers all the way from Britain to Germany.

The exhaust pipes from the aircraft's engine stick out at the side.

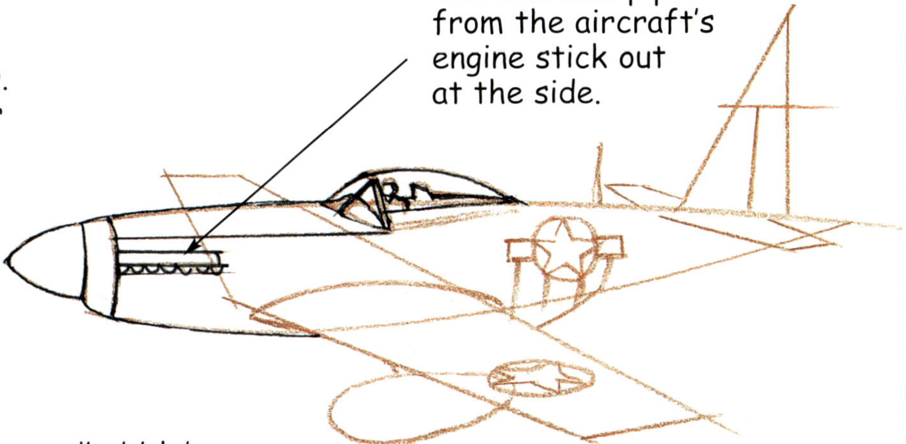

The cocktail has a 'bubble' canopy to give the pilot good all-round vision.

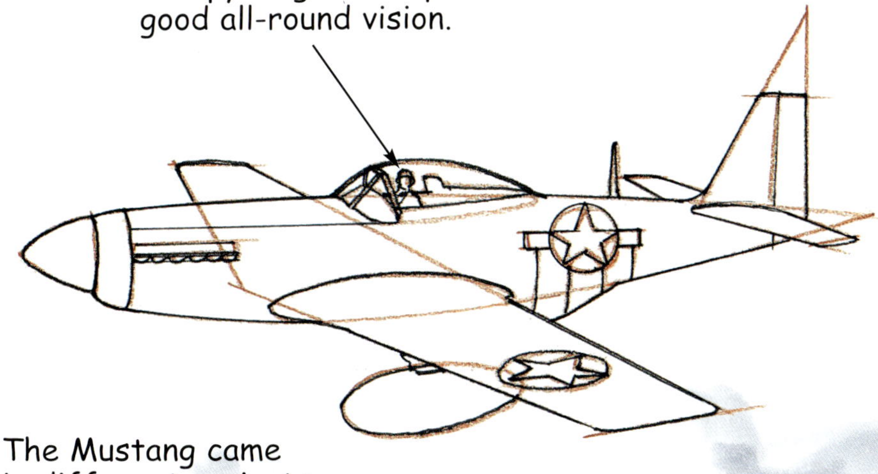

Early models had only four guns. Later versions had six guns and a supercharged engine. These later Mustangs destroyed more than 9,000 enemy aircraft.

The Mustang came in different variants as fighter, photo reconnaissance plane, or dive bomber.

Space Shuttle

First launched in 1981, the Space Shuttle is designed to travel repeatedly into space and back again – unlike earlier space rockets, which could be used only once.

A simple line and triangle form the basis of the Shuttle's three main sections: orbiter, rocket boosters, and external tank.

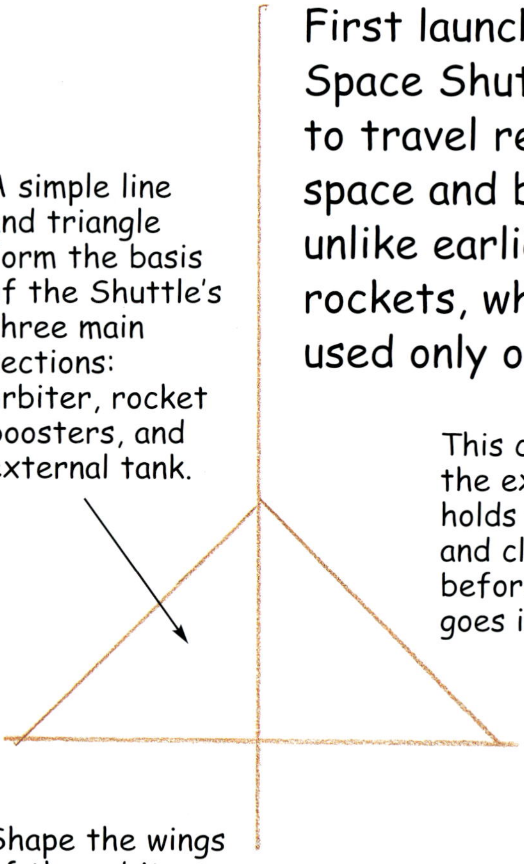

This column will form the external tank. It holds fuel for the launch and climb, and drops off before the Shuttle goes into orbit.

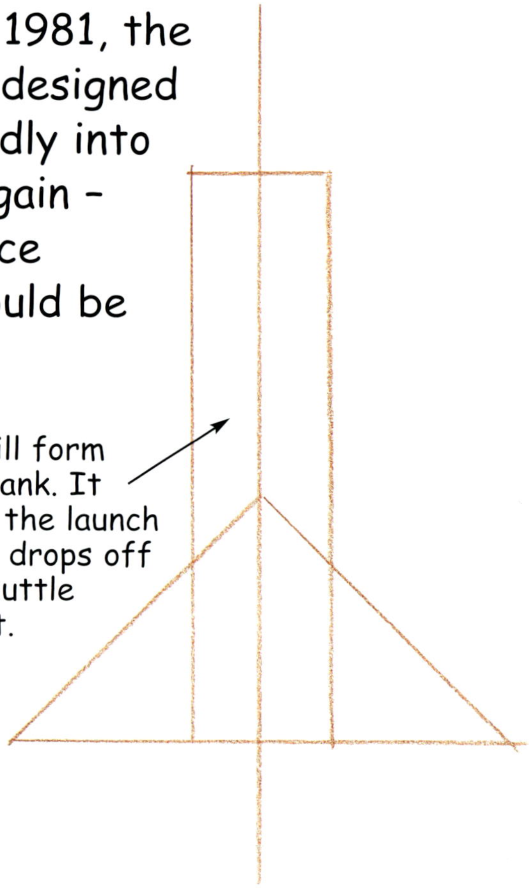

Shape the wings of the orbiter. These aid its return to Earth: it takes off like a rocket, but glides back like an airplane.

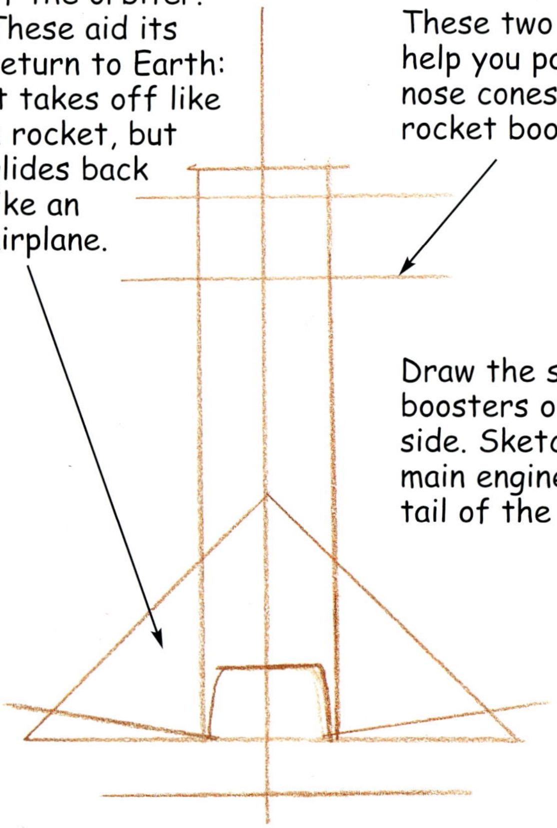

These two lines will help you position the nose cones of the rocket boosters.

Draw the slim rocket boosters on either side. Sketch in the main engines at the tail of the orbiter.

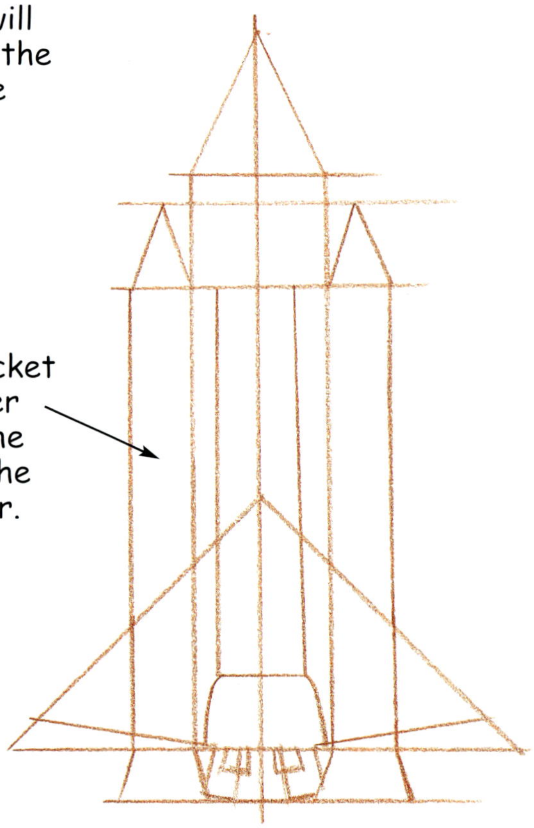

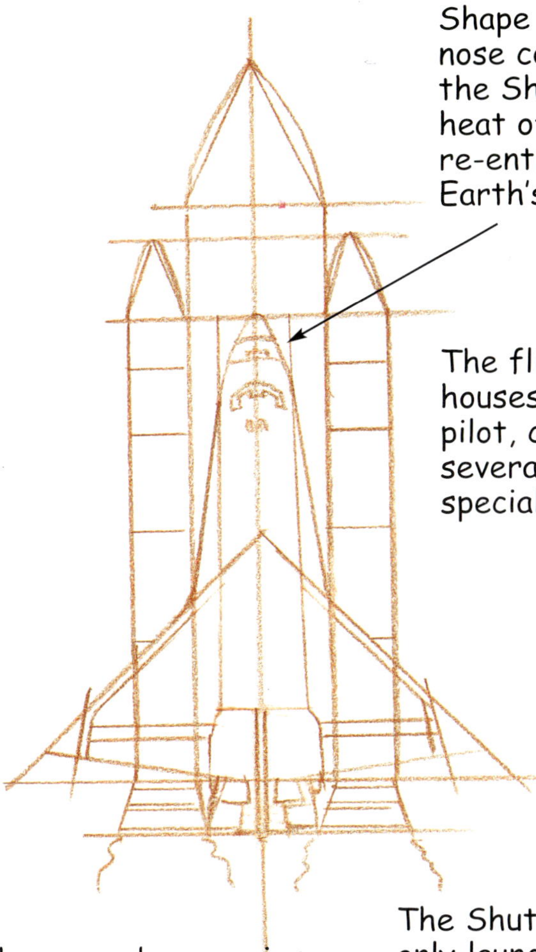

Shape the orbiter's nose cone. It protects the Shuttle against heat of 2300°F on re-entry into the Earth's atmosphere.

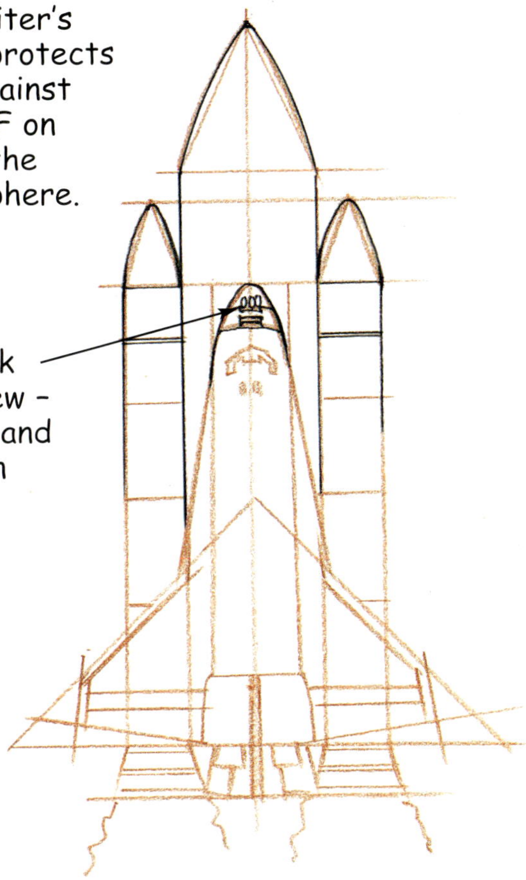

The flight deck houses the crew – pilot, co-pilot, and several mission specialists.

The cargo bay carries the payload – laboratories, telescopes and satellites etc.

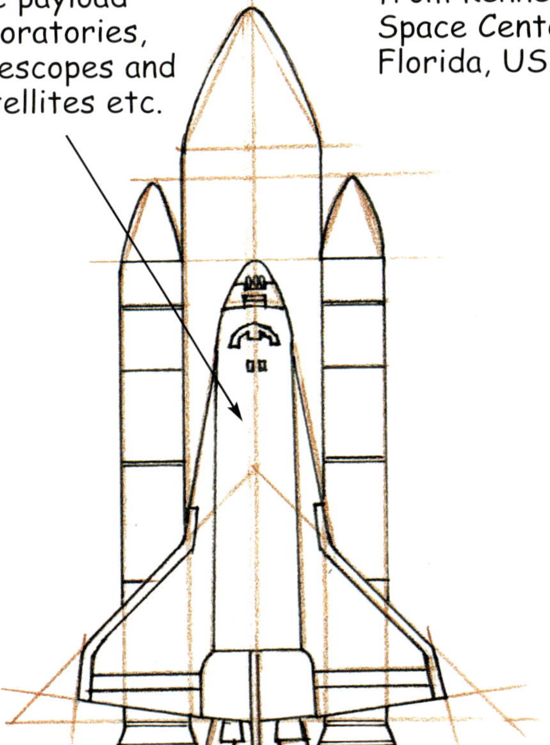

The Shuttle is only launched from Kennedy Space Center in Florida, USA.

Chinook Helicopter

In service since 1962, the Chinook is the standard medium transport helicopter of the US Army. It can carry up to 44 soldiers. It can also be used to transport cargo, which may be carried inside or slung underneath, with the helicopter acting as a flying crane.

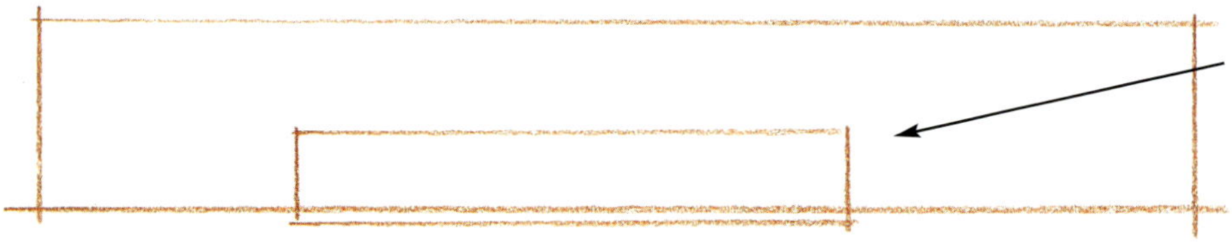

Start with a long box. Add a smaller box along the side - this is called a sponson, and contains fuel.

A block at each end forms rotor fairings. Instead of a large main rotor and smaller tail rotor, the Chinook has two main rotors sharing a drive shaft.

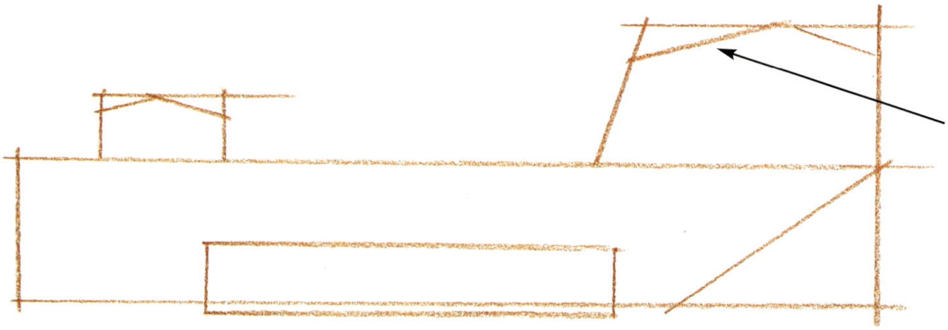

Use slanting lines to shape the tops of the rotor fairings, and cut off the back of the helicopter at an angle.

Draw the two rotors. These turn in opposite directions to keep the helicopter stable in the air.

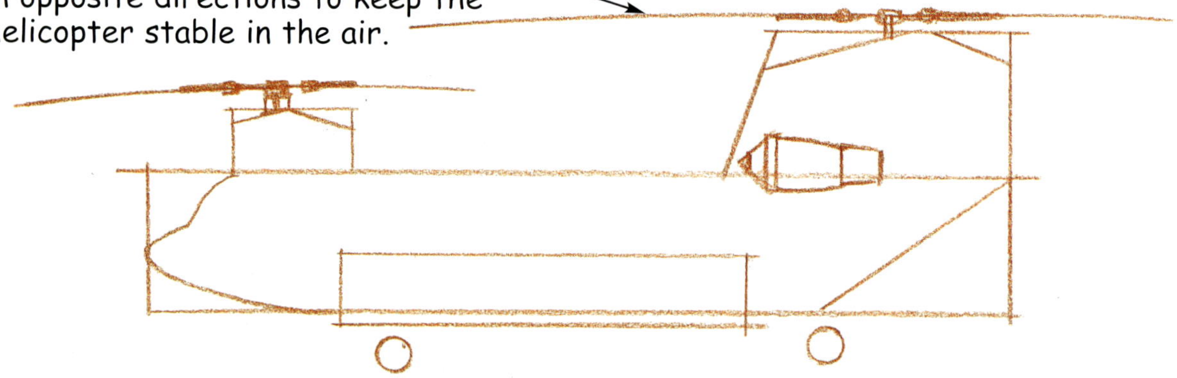

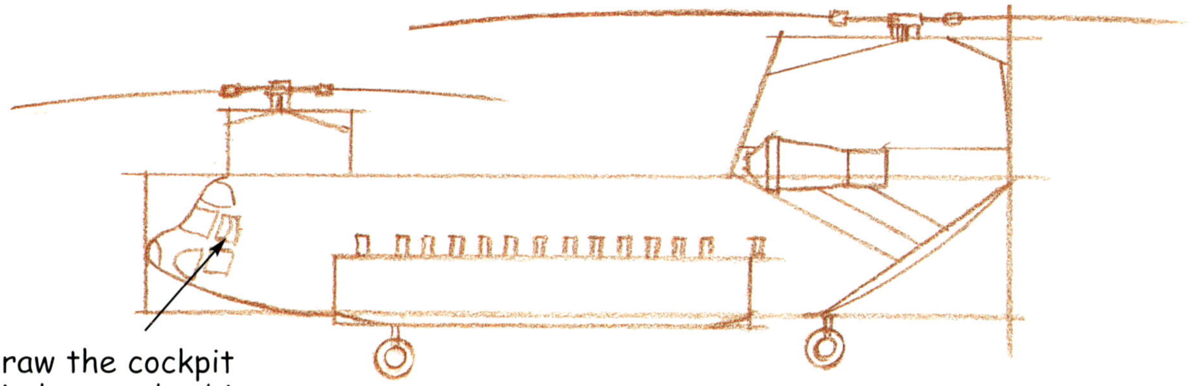

Draw the cockpit windows and cabin windows along the side.

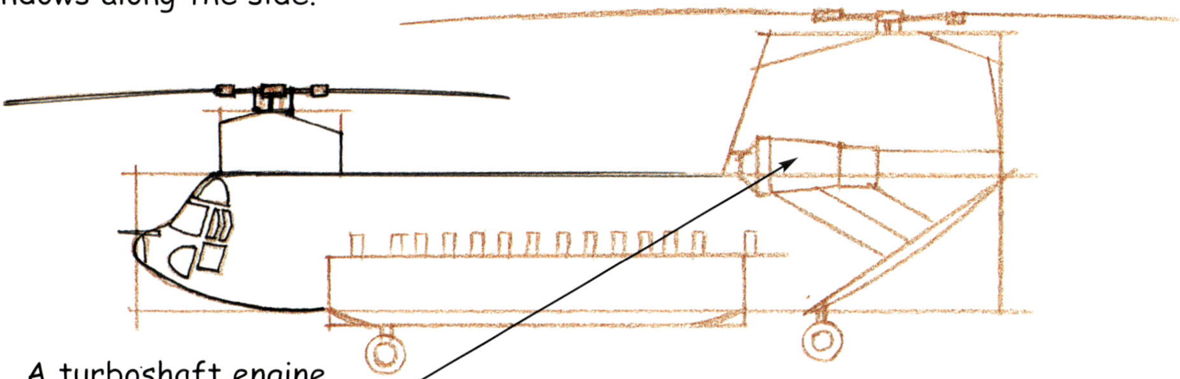

A turboshaft engine is fitted on each side of the tail.

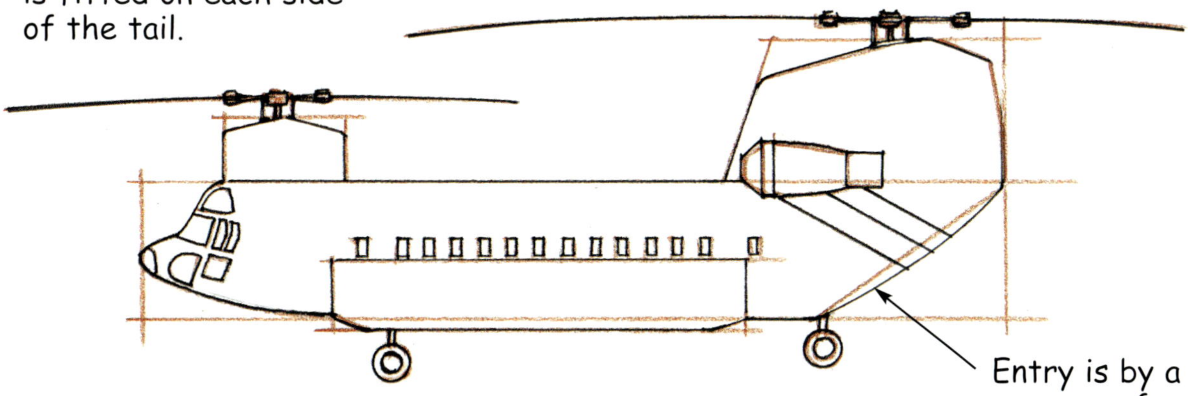

Entry is by a rear ramp, for easy loading of cargo or troops.

The Chinook can fly in all weathers. The fuselage is water-tight, so it can even land on water.

Microlight

This tiny aircraft is basically a hang glider with an engine. To support the motor, the structure has become a bit more complicated and the wing span has increased. The pilot has a seat instead of hanging from a harness.

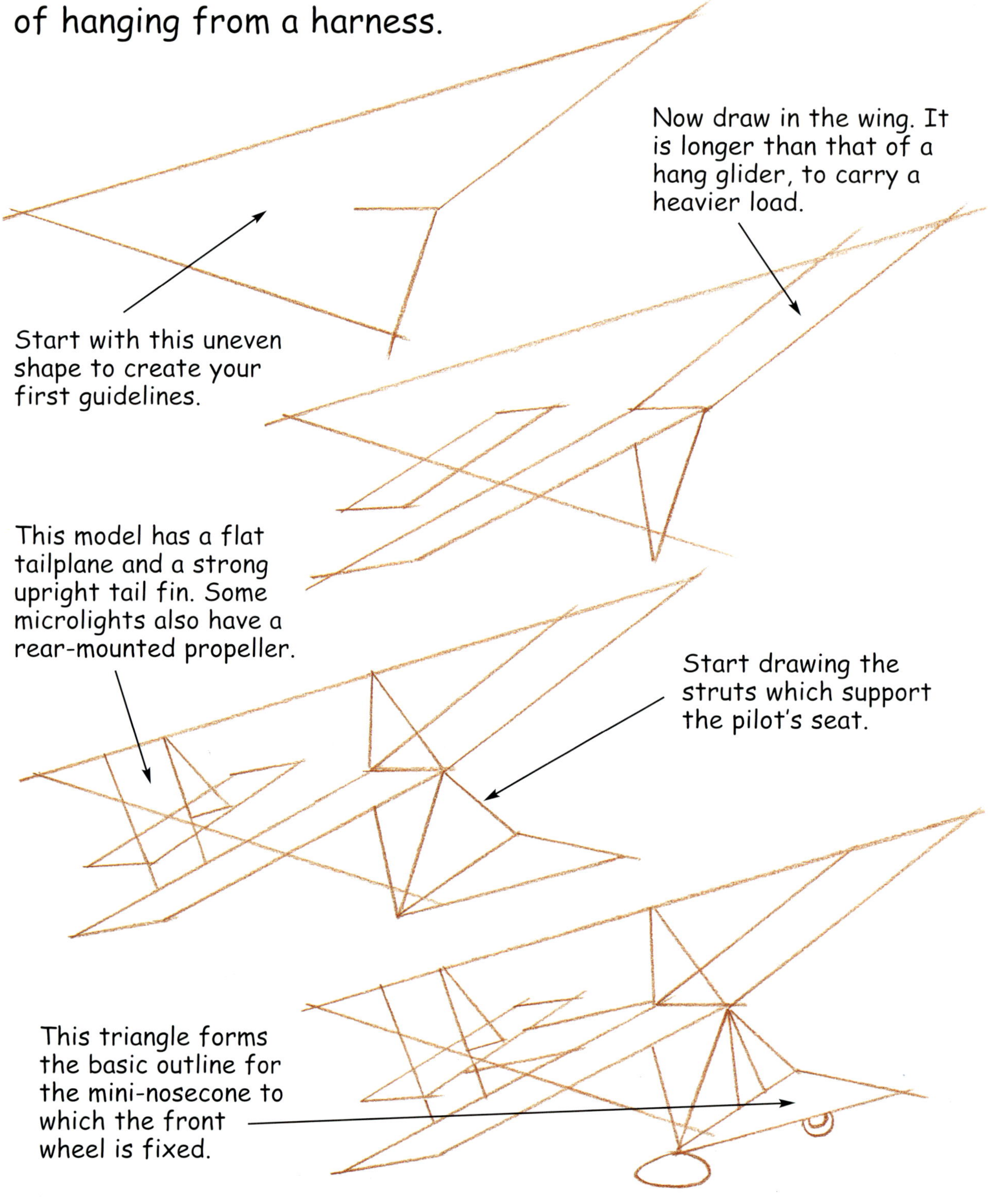

Mark in bands across the wing.

The engine, mounted just under the wing, is not much bigger than a lawnmower's.

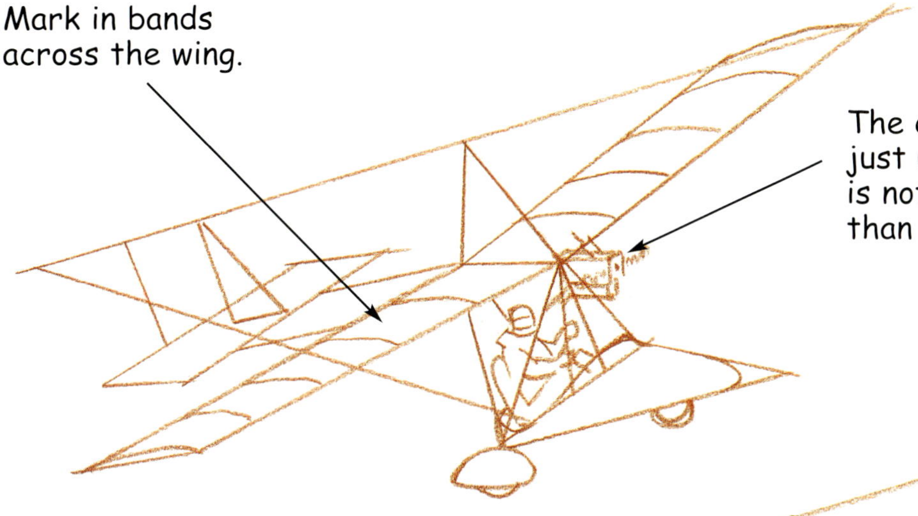

Microlights first appeared in 1976, when a hang glider was fitted with a small engine and propeller. At first, would-be pilots made their own. Then kits became available for home-building.

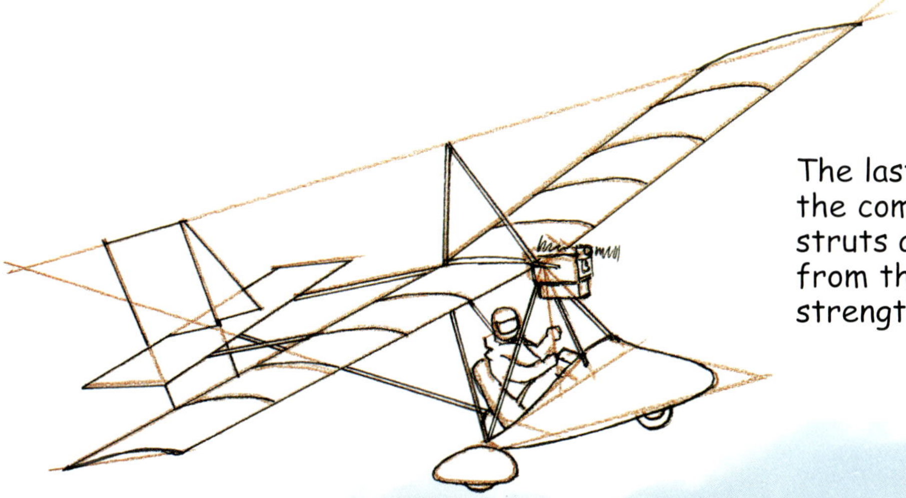

The last stage is to fill in the complicated system of struts and wires that run from the central mast to strengthen the structure.

Modern microlights have a cruising speed of between 30 and 60mph. In 1986–87, a lady pilot flew her microlight all the way from England to Australia.

Spitfire

The most famous fighter plane of all time, the Spitfire first flew in 1936. Its nimble handling made it popular with Britain's RAF pilots as they took on enemy aircraft during World War II.

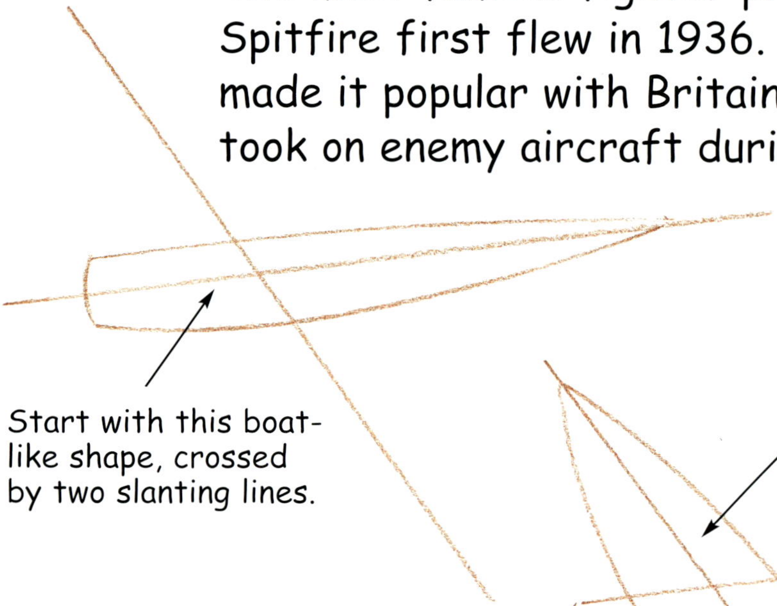

Start with this boat-like shape, crossed by two slanting lines.

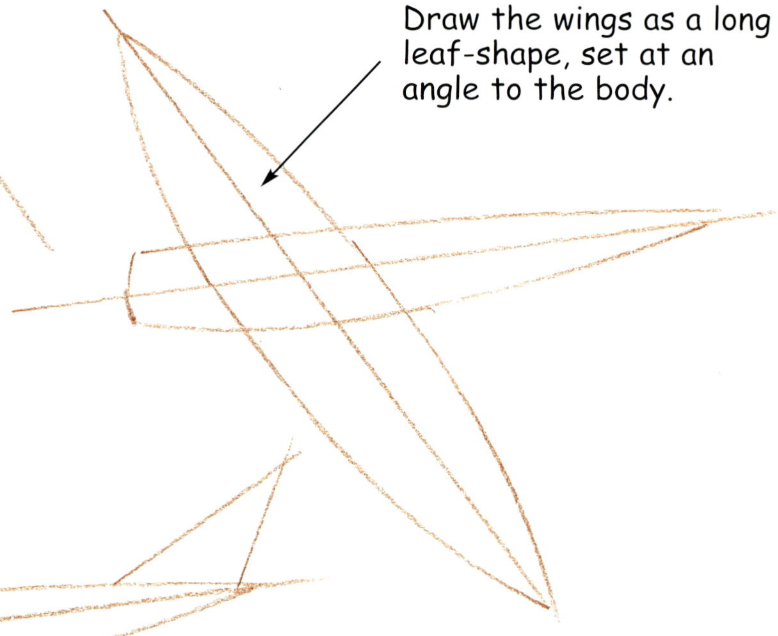

Draw the wings as a long leaf-shape, set at an angle to the body.

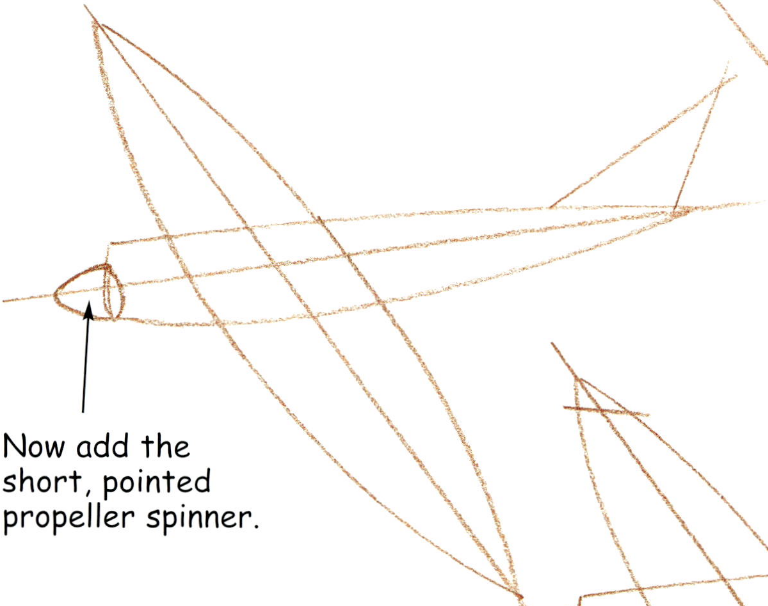

Now add the short, pointed propeller spinner.

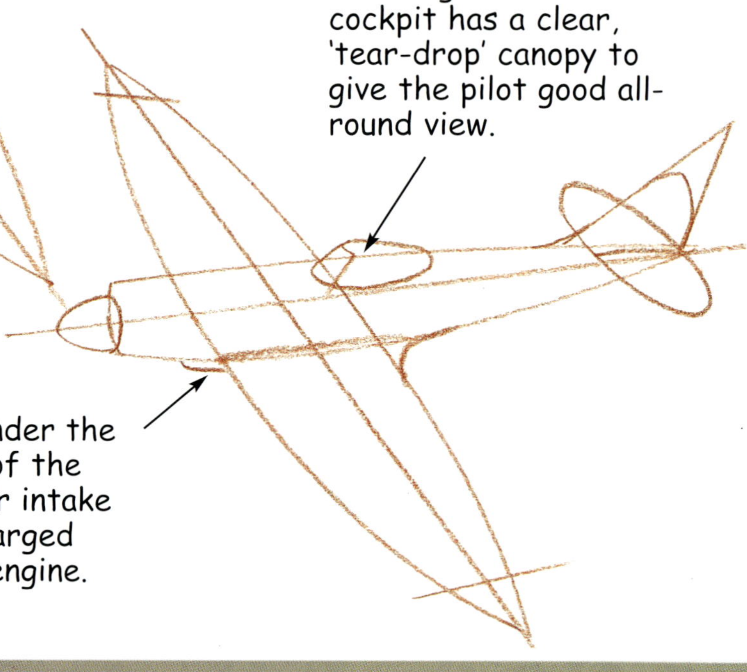

The single-seater cockpit has a clear, 'tear-drop' canopy to give the pilot good all-round view.

Add a little bump under the body, just in front of the wings. This is the air intake to cool the supercharged Rolls-Royce Merlin engine.

The Spitfire was light, fast and easy to fly; it made an ideal fighter.

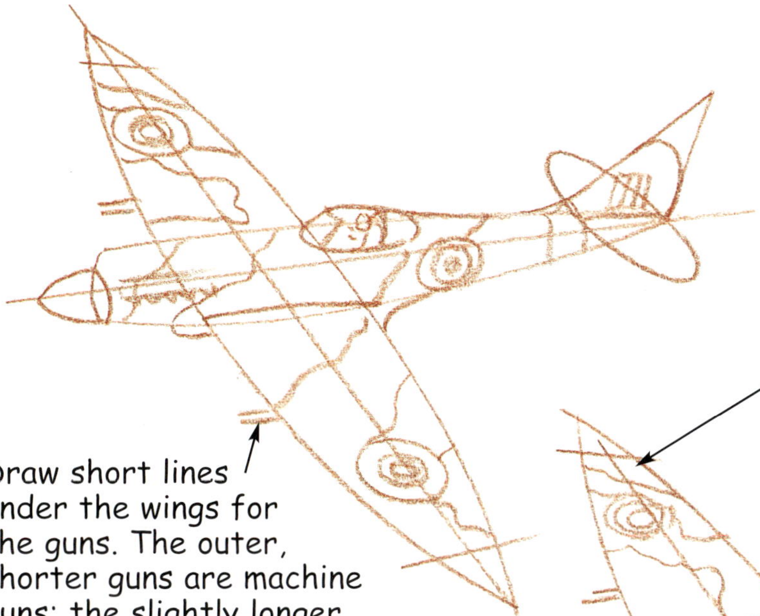

Draw short lines under the wings for the guns. The outer, shorter guns are machine guns; the slightly longer inner ones are cannon firing more powerful shells.

Round off the edges of the wings. Machine guns and ammunition are mounted inside the wings.

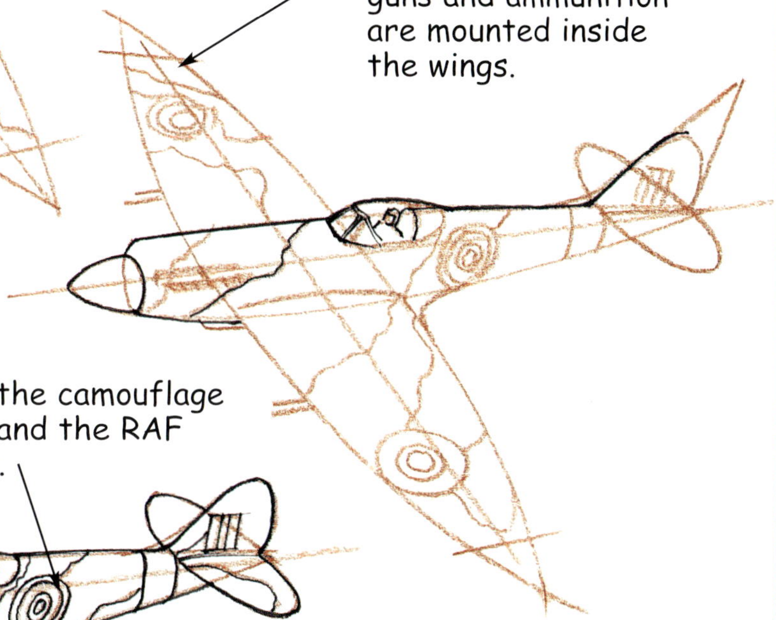

Draw in the camouflage pattern and the RAF roundels.

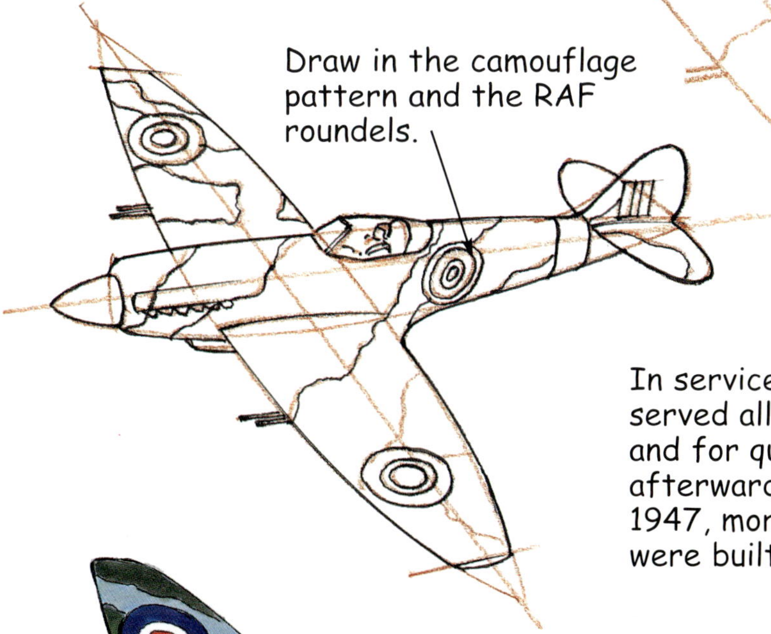

In service from 1939, the Spitfire served all through World War II and for quite a long time afterwards. Between 1939 and 1947, more than 20,000 Spitfires were built for the RAF.

Supermarine Seaplane

The Supermarine is a seaplane, with floats instead of wheels so that it can land on or take off from water. In the late 1920s, when the Supermarine was built, it was the fastest plane in the world. It was designed specially to compete in an annual race called the Schneider Trophy.

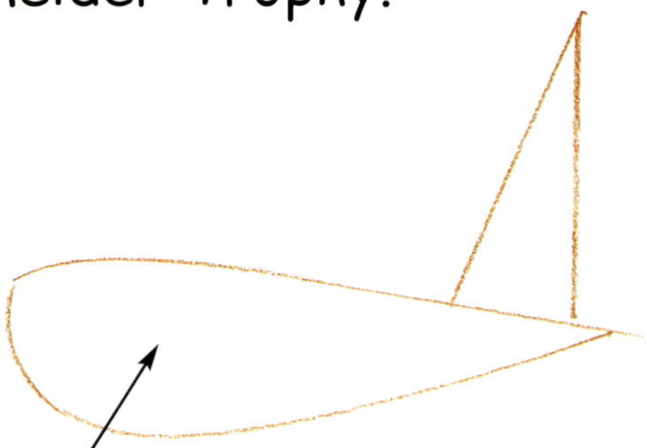

Start with this shape, blunt at one end and pointed at the other. Add a big, tall tail fin.

These two triangles at the base form the struts which attach the floats (also known as pontoons) to the body.

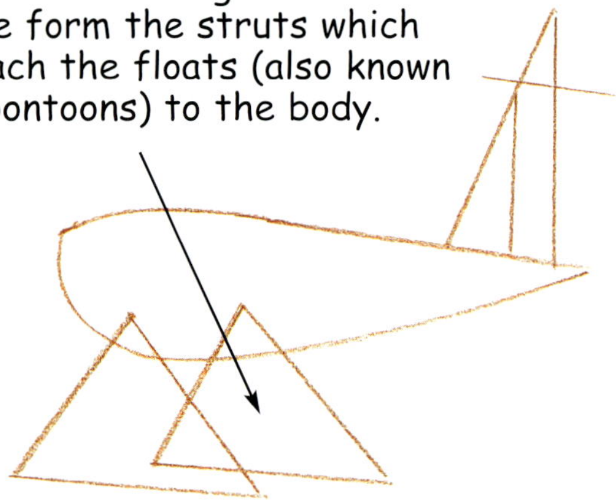

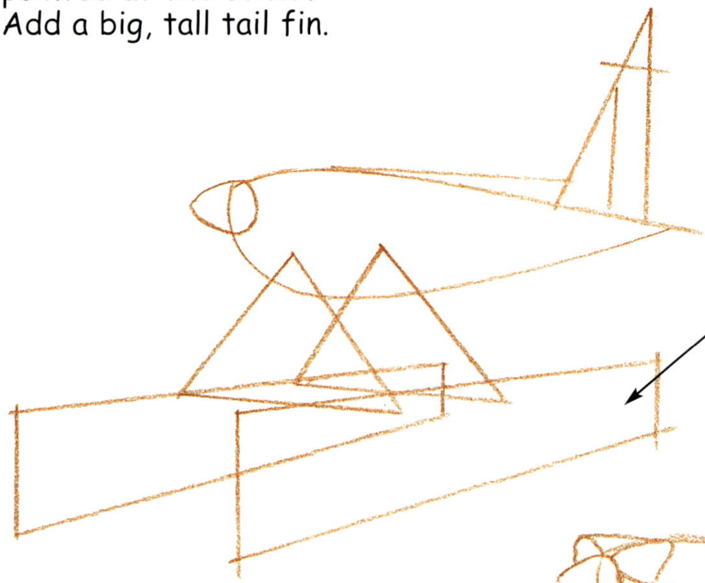

Under your triangles, add these two long rectangle shapes, as deep as the body, to form guidelines for the floats.

Now draw in the large, canoe-shaped floats. These hold the seaplane above the water.

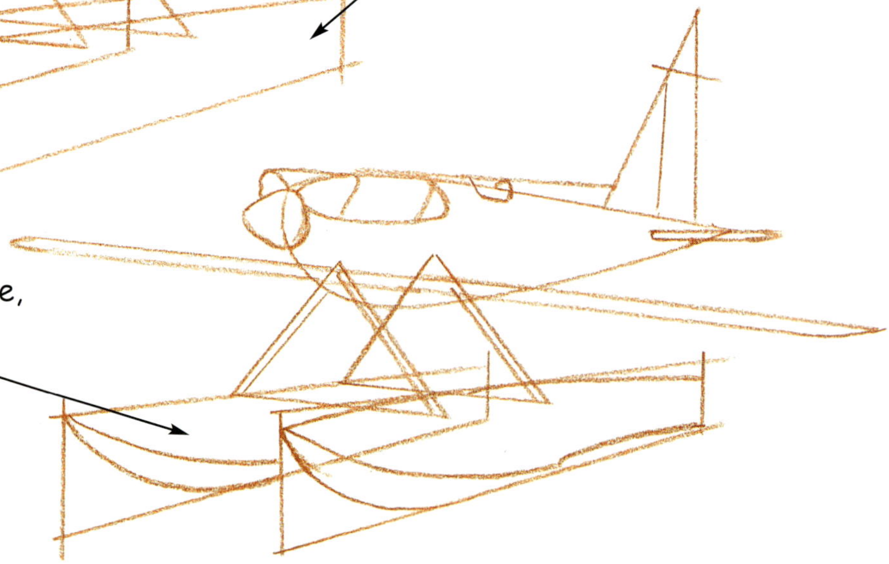

Finish drawing the floats, using curved lines to develop the shape.

The pilot sits well back, almost at the center of the aircraft, in the open cockpit of this single-seater.

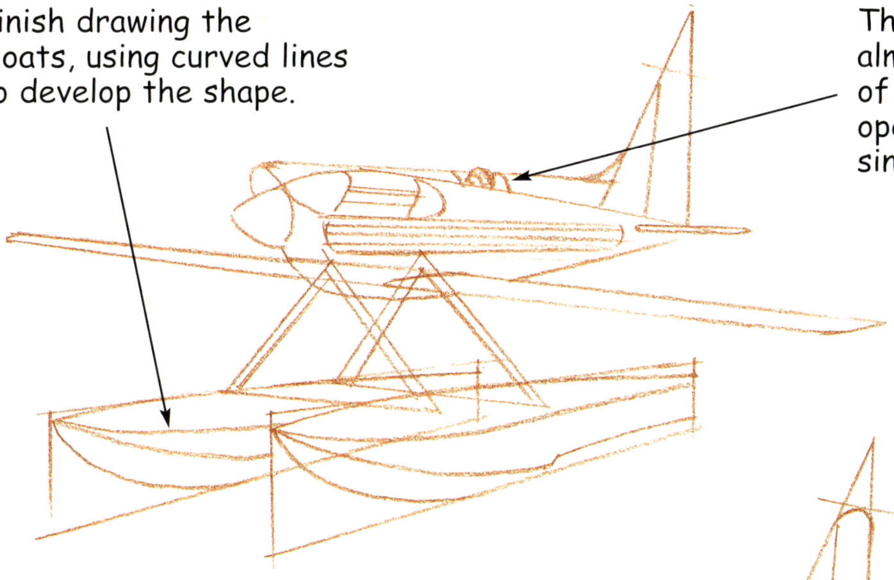

In 1931, the Supermarine set the first 400mph-plus speed record – two weeks after winning the Schneider Trophy race for Britain.

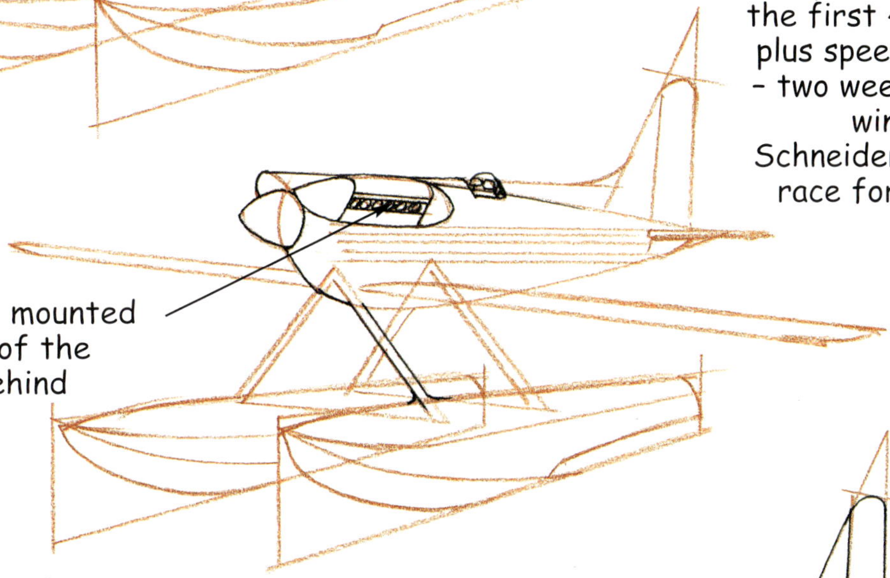

The engine is mounted at the front of the plane, just behind the nose.

Ink in your lines, contrasting the chunky body and floats with the slender struts, wings and tailplane.

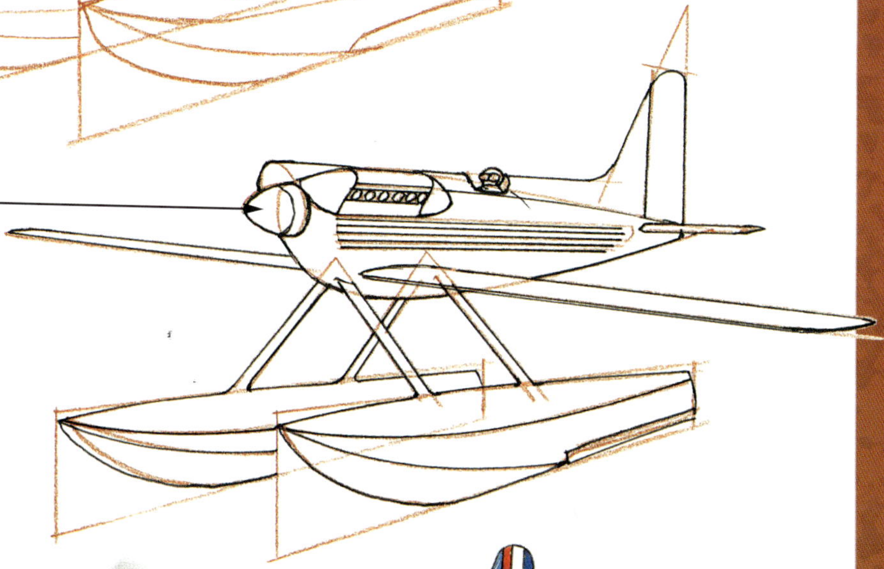

This Supermarine design was the basis for the famous Spitfire fighter of World War II.